MEMOIRS

OF

The Principal Events

IN THE

LIFE OF HENRY TAYLOR,

OF NORTH SHIELDS:

WHEREIN ARE INTERSPERSED THE

CIRCUMSTANCES THAT LED TO THE FIXING OF
LIGHTS IN HASBORO' GATT, THE
GODWIN, AND SUNK SANDS.

"AS WE HAVE THEREFORE OPPORTUNITY LET US DO GOOD UNTO ALL MEN." PAUL.

North Shields:

SOLD BY DARTON AND HARVEY, GRACE-CHURCH STREET;
AND VERNOR, HOOD, AND SHARPE, POULTRY,
LONDON.

1811.

PREFACE.

It was many years after the memoirs were written before I had any intention to print them: they were written for the instruction of my sons, who were sailors, to point out to them their duty as men and as christians; and it is more than probable they would never have met the public eye, but finding afterwards that they were connected with, and may be considered as a preface to, the circumstances that led to the fixing of the lights in Hasboro' Gatt, the Goodwin, and Sunk Sands, I was advised to print the whole.

The first part may not appear very interesting, yet it is presumed the young sailor may find some useful counsel and caution; and when he finds how a youth with little school learning and without any connections capable of assisting him in regard to promotion; that after his apprenticeship, he served only two voyages afore-the-mast, and that he commanded a large ship in the twenty-first year of his age—the emulous young sailor may hope for similar preferment, if he pursue the same means.

The shipping and commercial interests are much interested in the events that succeeded the year 1789, by which they have been benefited to a vast amount annually, as was predicted at the time, and which has been verified by an experience of more than twenty years.

I had once thought of writing the memoirs in the third person, to avoid the charge of egotism; but, considering that my letters, which are necessarily introduced, were written and signed by myself, and all letters on the subject of the lights were addressed to me, I thought it more consistent with the unity of my design to appear in my proper person.

I have not been very solicitous about the choice of language, but have endeavoured to write the whole in that plain stile I am accustomed to use in common conversation, and to represent facts as they really were; and conscious of having done so, I rely on the candour of the public.

As the work principally concerns sea-faring men, I have thought it unnecessary to explain the technical terms of seamanship, because they are so well understood by sailors; nor have I been very ceremonious with regard to the Trinity House; but if any one think I have been too severe in my remarks on their conduct, he will find sufficient cause in the corporation's false statements, and in their contemptuous treatment of me. It has always been my maxim, " To love all men, and fear none."

That all (especially the rising generation of seamen), who read my memoirs, may receive essential benefit, is the sincere prayer of the

SAILOR's FRIEND,

HENRY TAYLOR.

5th Mo. 1811.

MEMOIRS.

I was born in a sea-port town, in the north of England, in the year 1737; and as most boys in such situations incline towards a sea-faring life, I always had a strong inclination for it; and notwithstanding the entreaties of a tender parent, to choose a less dangerous employment, I could not be prevailed on. About the thirteenth year of my age, I was bound an apprentice, for the term of six years. I had a good master; but mates, and even common sailors in those days, were very strict with boys, kept them close confined on board, and used various means to raise in them a desire to excel, by assigning degrading employments to those that were latest in turning out, or were any way careless or unhandy in doing their duty.

This strictness, provided no unnecessary severity is used, seems requisite, because the preservation of ship and people on board very often depend on attention and quick exertion. I served my apprenticeship faithfully, chiefly in the coal trade, but we were during the time two voyages to Stockholm, and one to Norway.

In one of the Stockholm voyages we delivered our cargo of tar in the wet dock or bason at Portsmouth, when on a sudden the ship began to bounce so that the whole crew were alarmed, they were afraid she would break all her moorings; although it was nearly calm, the water in the bason ran about six feet up the sides; and the ships building near us trembled like leaves shaken with the wind.

This proved to be the same earthquake that desolated Lisbon, and buried so many thousands in its ruins.

From my first going to sea, I fully expected that I should soon after the expiration of my apprenticeship be a master; and knowing that none of my relations were in a capacity to help me to any preferment, and that I must depend for success on my own merit, I applied myself closely to learn every part of a seaman's duty.

As the ship lay by two or three months in winter, I went to school during that time, learned navigation, and was able to keep a ship's way before I had been four years at sea.

In 1756, I was a free man. I was vain, and not altogether free from other vices, yet not at that early period destitute of the knowledge of a divine and internal monitor, the reproofs of which I often felt, and the justness of which I often acknowledged in tenderness and tears.

In 1757, I made one coal and one Baltic voyage afore-the-mast, which were the only two I ever made in that capacity.

As some curious occurences were attendant on the said Baltic voyage, and as some useful reflections may be drawn therefrom, I shall mention some of them.

The ship in which I engaged belonged to Hull, was then loading coals at Shields for Lubec, and bound from thence to Riga, to load timber for Hull; there were several men in this ship afore-the-mast, and they were all young. The captain was one who indulged himself in bed during night in every situation: the mate, a middle aged man, was much addicted to strong liquor. Nothing material happened on the passage between Shields and the Sound, where having cleared, and got our stock of spirits on board we proceeded; it fell dark soon after passing Draco, and the master (as his custom was) went to sleep, and left the ship to the care of the chief-mate, who presently invited me and the other young men in his watch to drink grog with him, by which we thought ourselves honored, and we gave him so freely of ours, that in a short time he fell stupidly drunk down into the steerage. The wind was at W. or W. N. W. and blew fresh. We were at a loss what to do. We could not think of acquainting the master, and therefore as some of us had been up the Baltic, we resolved to run the ship on until the watch was out, which we did safely, so that when the second-mate came on deck, she was nearly a breast of Moon Island, and in a fair way.

During the remainder of the voyage there happened frequent quarrels between the captain and the mate; the former was proud and supercilious, and the latter, though he knew his duty, was a drunken negligent man.

On returning from Riga, and turning through between the Dwall Grounds, and the main, with a press of wind, the master was so inconsiderate as to go to sleep. It was night, standing in for the land at the rate of five or six knots; the mate, standing on the windlass-end, fell asleep; a young man at the helm, who had often been at Riga, said to me, " We are running too far in;" I immediately snatched up the lead, and finding little more than three fathoms, cried out, " Hard-a-lee, Tom." The helm was immediately put down, the sea being smooth, the ship came quickly about; but so stupidly drunk and asleep was the mate, that we were hauling the head yards about before he awoke.

From this and the circumstance of leaving the ship to the care of a few unexperienced lads, between Draco and Falsterborn, one need not wonder that so many ships are lost: for, doubtless, what happened during this voyage may and does often happen. It is certainly the duty of such as see them to make them known, and not, from false notions of humanity, to hide the mate's bad conduct from the master, as I and the other young men did; although we believed the second mate did if so, the master was inexcuseable in leaving the care of the ship to so improper a person. Such masters and mates are unworthy of command. Men in those stations should not only be sober, but vigilent and watchful, since they are not only charged with the ship and cargo, but with the lives of all that sail with them. What a dreadful account will such careless masters have to give at the last day!

On arrival at Hull, the master discharged both chief and second mate, and made me his chief mate; but the old mate, out of revenge, informed the press-gang (for it was then war) that I had not been chief-mate the voyage; they therefore took me out of the ship, and put me into the hold of a tender, where I lay near a month, and was cleared, only, by getting a man in my stead.

This voyage was also to Riga; it proved a very severe one. We were near a month in the East Sea; often under reefed courses, long nights, and very cold weather.

At this time I had keen convictions. The petulence of the captain, increased by the storms and contrary winds we met with, often drew from me sharp and angry replies, for which, especially during night, I felt bitter repentance, and formed resolutions to observe a more respectful conduct.

Late in the year we arrived at Hull, and I left the ship to spend the winter with my aged mother.

In the spring of 1758, I went a voyage mate of a ship to Riga, and delivered our cargo at my native place. Nothing remarkable happened on this voyage. The captain of this ship and I did not very well agree; I therefore left her; but I did not consider what I had to suffer by being seen on shore in the middle of summer, of which I soon grew weary; for I was ashamed to be seen by any that knew me, and would have been glad to have gone any where, in any situation. I had not been long on shore, when the owner of a transport engaged me to go second mate, which I thankfully accepted, and went with the owner's son to Portsmouth where the ship lay. Here the chief mate left her, and I was preferred to that station. In a few days the ship was ordered round to Deptford and discharged from government service. The captain then left her, not choosing to go in the coal trade. I was now in the twenty-first year of my age made master of a large ship, this was highly flattering to my vanity, of which I had a large share, but which I was enabled to sacrifice to prudence and a sense of my inexperience. I therefore wrote to the owner, that I thought myself too young to take charge of so large a ship as the Mary, and requested he would procure a master to meet me at Shields, and I would serve him in the capacity of mate.

During the remainder of this year, the ship continued in the coal trade; and it was now that I became remarkably serious. I had heard but little preaching, or had little converse with men on the subject of religion. The divine light (a measure of which I believe was given to every man) was my instructor; and I proved its sufficicency, by being led by it into great poverty of spirit, and deadness of the world's pleasures. I looked on every created good as unworthy a christian's notice, and went to an extreme in self-denial respecting meats, drinks, and apparel, for which some did, doubtless, blame me, but which I considered necessary.

In the fore-part of 1760, the Mary was again taken into the service of government, and I was again made master of her. In this year I made two trips to the river Weeser with troopers' horses. The remainder of the year we lay up in the river Thames.

During the time I lay at Deptford, I became acquainted with the people called Methodists, with whom I associated: and, although I never could accord with them in some particulars, I saw no people evidence so much zeal for the salvation of mankind; and it was this, rather than their opinions, that united me to them; nor were the Methodists in those days, like most other sects, strongly attached to a particular system: their particular design was to do good to to all as they had opportunity.

After I left their society I did not cease to love them, nor could I ever hear them degradingly spoken of without being grieved; and often have I reproved the ignorance of foolish men when I have heard them thus traduced.

Having now the command of a large ship, in which were seventeen or eighteen men and boys, I considered them all as committed to my care by Divine Providence. I discouraged all immorality, and instructed the ship's company, as well as I was able, in their duty to God and man and in this I had such success! that an oath was rarely heard on board. I treated the men with so much tenderness that few left me but with regret.

I seldom punished boys, but expected prompt obedience from them, as well as from the men, which was rendered by them with cheerfulness; because I never commanded any thing but what it was their duty to do.

Early in 1761, I was ordered from Deptford to Portsmouth, where the ship was filled with fascines and gabions, for the purpose of temporary batteries, with which we sailed to Belisle, on the coast of France, thence to Plymouth and shortly afterwards from Plymouth to Cork; between which place and Belisle-road I was employed in carrying live bullocks and sheep until the end of the year.

During the several voyages to and from the coast of France, we were often without company: I had frequent reasonings in my mind about fighting; and often said to my mate, "It would be a sad thing, if, in defending ourselves, we should kill others. We must, in case we meet a privateer, fire at her masts and rigging, and so disable her, as to give us an opportunity of running from her;" to which my mate agreed, we being of similar sentiments on this subject.

It must give pain to a reflecting mind to know that this ship belonged to one of the people called Quakers, who in their society capacity have always borne an uniform testimony against war, defensive as well as offensive, for which many individuals have experienced deep sufferings; but the owner of this ship entered freely into the business of war, from motives of temporal interest. O self interest! thou art the god of this world, and almost all the world doth worship thee!

As hinted before, I always kept up a strict discipline without severity. I taught my boys to fear the Almighty, to love one another, to avoid lying, swearing, and to copy after the most expert seamen, to strive to cat the anchor, to haul out the weather-earing, and on every general call to endeavour to be foremost.

Amongst the seamen, I discouraged drunkenness, quarreling, and swearing; so that those disorders so common in most ships, were rarely seen or heard of in that which I commanded. Whenever I got any new men, I took an early opportunity to inform them, that I admitted no cursing, swearing, or the like, in my ship; that I would as long as they sailed with me treat them with tenderness and humanity; but unless they governed themselves by the rules which I had prescribed, I would take the first opportunity of discharging them: and it was very remarkable, that however much such seamen had been addicted to those practices, they forbore them whilst they sailed with me, without any apparent constraint put upon them. So docile are the generality of seamen, and so easily drawn to that which is good.

If boys were inattentive to, or unhandy in, doing their duty, I endeavoured to make them ashamed, by saying, " I was afraid I should have no credit of them," or, " That I should never be able to make them good sailors." This had a more powerful effect than blows could possibly have, which are often inflicted from caprice or passion, more than from any demerit in the party punished.

Men who have a sense of religion, should let none excel them in care and diligence. They that fear God can do more than others, especially in time of danger and difficulty, when the hearts of wicked men generally fail them, and their understandings become clouded and confused,—Not so the good man

—he fears the Almighty, and thinks there is nothing else which he ought to fear.

Before we proceed further, it may be of use to mention a few anecdotes, to shew that my zeal for religion did not enfeeble my mind, cause me to neglect my duty as a seaman, or forget the respect due to my situation; but in which, however, are discoverable some traces of pride, and youthful vanity.

In one of the voyages to Bellisle, our ship was riding in a clear birth, when a sloop of war came to anchor close under our stern; the captain of which called to me to get out of the way immediately. Piqued at the supercilious pride of this servant of the public, I answered him, perhaps too smartly, "If I should now take up my anchor, our ship will fall athwart your hause: I had a clear birth before you gave me a foul one; but I have more regard for the property committed to my care, than to lay so near any ship, and shall certainly move to a greater distance as soon as the tide makes to windward."

Offended at such an answer, the captain sent an officer and boat's crew on board, to see the ship got under way, and on his getting on the quarter-deck, he took me by the collar. Two or three friends who had come on board to see me, fired at such insolence in the officer, were about to use him ill, which I prevented; but at the same time told my people to take hold of the officer, and turn him over the side into his own boat, which they did, without hurting him. He returned soon after, in greater force. By this time the tide was making to windward, and the people were heaving the ship to her anchor. The mate was in his place on the windlass, they took him off, and carried him on board the sloop of war. On getting our ship into a proper birth, I went on board to demand my mate, which the captain of the sloop of war refused to comply with. I then went to our old agent, Captain Randall (who was a real friend to the masters of transports, and was much respected by them) and told him the case. He bid me go to the captain of the sloop, and tell him, that if he did not immediately liberate my mate, he would report him to Commodore Keppel. On delivering this message, the mate was discharged.

I usually took with me, from Cork, a number of religious pamphlets, which I distributed amongst the poor soldiers and sailors; this brought me into the notice of many of their officers.

In Basque Road I was respectfully noticed by many naval officers, particularly on board the commodore, Sir Thomas Stanhope. Once dining in the ward-room, one of the officers swore, but immediately looking towards me, asked my pardon. The Priest was sitting at the same table, but he no doubt had been accustomed to hear them without reproving them.

It happened once when in Basque Road that a gale of wind came on right into the bay; there were riding many ships of war, and several transports; the commodore made signal for striking topmasts, which was obeyed by all but one transport, and she rode the weather-most ship. It blew very hard and the sea ran high; the commodore was much offended at the captain, who kept his topmasts up; for if his anchors or cables had given way he might have been the cause of the loss of many ships and lives. As they could not tell on board the commodore the transport's name, they supposed it might be me; who had faith to believe I could ride as long with topmasts up as others with their's down; and the officers, many of whom respected me, were sorry I should be so presumptuous. How natural is it for men to annex some absurdity or other to the character of religious persons, than which nothing can be more foolish. My notions of religion preserved me from many ridiculous absurdities, that I saw others fall into. If a man's religion be of the genuine kind, he will be careful to fulfil all the relative duties of life; and it will be his constant endeavour "To keep a conscience void of offence towards God, and towards man."

On the gale abating, and the sea tolerably smooth, the commodore made signal for all masters of transports. I always made it a point to be very attentive to orders; and in this case, was one of the first on board. Before I got to the gang-way, several of the officers shook their heads, and said, "Taylor, we are very sorry you should have behaved as you have done, the commodore is very angry at you." "For what?" said I; "What have I done?" "For keeping up your top-masts, when every other ship had them down. Is not that your ship to windward?" I answered, " No; there she lays, and her top-masts were down with the first."

The officers were very glad to find that it was so; and candidly said, they suspected it was me, for the reasons already given. The offending master* was, I believe, severely reprimanded by the commodore.

During the several voyages which we made from Cork to Belisle and Basque Road, with bullocks and sheep, I had many opportunities of trafficing to great advantage; but being in a manner dead to the desire of gain, I made use of those opportunities for the advantage of others. I took out ventures of blocks, shoes, linen, soap, candles, &c. for poor religious tradesmen, which I sold and brought them good returns. I also executed commissions for masters of transports, for live stock, butter, potatoes, &c. for which I never took more than prime cost; and often carried out fowls, geese, &c. on purpose to give away: for I seldom indulged myself in any thing better than the common fare of the ship, tea excepted. I rarely

* John Broderick, ship Enterprize, of Newcastle.

carried wine or spirits in the ship for any other purpose than to give to others.

Whilst the ship lay at Cork I frequently dined with the richer methodists, friends, and others, and was in those visits generally accompanied by a particular acquaintance*.' We were often burthened with the luxury of their tables, especially their immoderate use of wine; and the matter lay so weightily upon our minds, that we resolved to commence drinking water only; and thus, by example, reproved unnecessary indulgence in others.

Eating and drinking so coarsely and sparingly was too severe a discipline for my hitherto good constitution: a pleuritic fever seized me, on our passage from the coast of France to Cork, which place we could not fetch, and therefore put into Crook-haven, about fifty miles to the south-west of Cork. No doctor could be found near this barren and inhospitable place; and as I judged from the violent spasms in my right side, that bleeding was necessary, that operation was performed five times by a plowman. In a few days the fever abated,

* John Helton, then of Cork, but now resident at Bristol.

my cough moderated, and I began to desire some nourishment; for during the time the fever was on me, I took nothing but a sharp mixture to break the cough.

It may be proper in this place to mention the fidelity of an Irish lad, (my cabin boy) one of my apprentices. During the whole time the fever lasted, this lad would not leave me night or day, nor let any one sit up with him. As I sweat profusely, he kept airing me shirts and night caps. One night finding my cough very troublesome, and my breast much closed, without any advice, or instruction, he made up a mixture of honey, vinegar, and probably some other ingredients, brought it to me, and desired me to take a little of it, which I did, and found great relief from it.

The first thing I inclined to eat was apples; but no such thing was on board, nor any to be had in the neighbourhood. Francis, for that was the boy's name, determined his master should have apples, if he travelled as far as Cork for them. He set off for the country; how far he went I do not know, but he could find no person who had any to sell. At last, distressed no doubt at his ill success, he saw at a distance a gentleman's house, to which he went; where making his case known, he obtained his hat full. These apples I ate raw and roasted, and recovered very fast.

From the relief received from bleeding, and from the good effects of the apples, I concluded that nature will generally point out what is most necessary; if men do but attend to its dictates: and I have often thought since, that people in fevers should have every thing they ask for, if not delirious.

At the end of the war, I was ordered to Deptford, where we arrived safe, and our ship was discharged from the service of government. I was ordered by the owner to Whitby, where the ship underwent a considerable repair.

In 1764, I was master of a ship called the Speedwell, of Whitby, and made that year one voyage to Norway, and one to Wyburg and London. I continued zealous for the promotion of religion, in practising it myself, and recommending it to others (especially those who sailed with me), and in every foreign port where I came I endeavoured to walk circumspectfully.

On our return from Wyburg, it was winter;

when we came on this coast, we fell in some where between the Dodgeon light and Cromer, but had not seen either of them, or the land. Night was approaching, and a gale of wind northerly; all the direction we had was from a fishing boat, or smack, that told us how he thought Cromer bore. It was not expected that we could keep to windward until morning; besides the decks were lumbered with deals, and the ship very tender. We were all in consternation, and I was very thoughtful. I went below a few moments, and returned on deck, with a mind impressed with a firm belief, that we should pass safely through. I then ordered the helm to be put a-weather; and fixed on such a course as I thought would run the ship through between Hasbro' Sand and the Lemon, which we did safely, and for which we were all truly thankful. At day light in the morning we saw many pieces of wreck, casks, &c. floating in the sea.

The way William Todd, who was then carpenter of the ship, told this occurrence to his friends, was as follows:

" Our situation was such, that we knew not what to do. The ship was laying to, and driving we knew not where. Our master went down to his cabin, and soon after returning on deck, told us, " To fear not, for it had been clearly made known to him, that not one hair of our heads should be hurt!"

It may not prove unprofitable to caution the reader against enthusiasm on the one hand, and scepticism on the other. To expect divine and immediate direction in all the trivial concerns of this life, is enthusiasm; and to suppose the Almighty does not attend to, and answer the earnest supplications of those that love and fear him, is deism or worse.

The case above-mentioned was a very momentous one. Finding my self destitute of all external guides; the lives of those in the ship with me in imminent danger of perishing; and, if they did perish, a censorious world imputing the loss to my ignorance, or perhaps even to my religion: is it to be wondered at, that in this extremity, I should, in an agony of prayer, cry out, " Lord save, or we perish:" or need we wonder, that when HE means to save, HE should impress the mind with an assurance of safety; and even point out the means to be made use of.

I had now attained the twenty-seventh year of my age. I continued several years longer at sea, was exposed to many dangers, and experienced singular deliverances, for which I was always thankful to the Great Preserver of Men.

In the winter of 1767, I sailed from Shields in company with fifteen sail; only six survived a dreadful storm, which came on soon after we got over the bar. It was on new year's day, the wind at first was due N. and continued so most of the night. The gale came on so heavy, that we handed all our sails, but the foresail. We attempted to steer an outwardly course, but we could not get the ship off from the wind; and therefore set down the fore tack, and ran off E. N. E. and E. all night. We could not conceive the reason why the ship would not steer; but in the morning we found that the tiller was broke in the rudder-head, which was a very providential circumstance, as it gave us such an offing, that though the gale was excessive, and the wind had veered during the night to N. E. and N. E. by E. we found ourselves in the morning abreast of Flambro' head, distant six miles.

During the night our boats, and every thing on deck, were washed overboard. The foresail, which had stood fast, now gave way, it was hauled up, and the crew went up to hand it; the mate* (a young man, whom I had recently preferred to that station, and for whom I had a particular respect) was on the weather yard-arm: the sail blew up, and threw him under it, so that he was in imminent danger every minute of dropping into the sea. I saw from the deck his perilous situation, and that none of the people attempted to save him; praying, in my heart that the Almighty would help me to rescue him, I flew up the shrouds, and firmly grasping the yard with my right arm, with the other I drew him to the shrouds, where the sailors were ready to receive and hold him fast.

With some difficulty we got the broken tiller out, and another put in, and then attempted to get the ship before the wind, to try for Bridlington Bay, in hopes that our anchors would hold, but to no purpose; she would not move off from the wind.

* Richard Hansell, living in North Shields at the time I am writing this

There was at this time a large ship belonging to Vickerman, of Scarborough, steering directly for us. Both pumps were at work; her sails were all in ribbands, and she appeared to be sinking; and they probably thought the only chance they had of saving their lives, was that of getting on board us. Vain hope! for if she had hit us, we had both gone to the bottom! She just missed our quarter; for when she came near, we put our helm a-weather, braced all the yards forward, and our ship providentially got head-way, and by that means avoided the fatal stroke.

We had now little hope of keeping off the land until morning. A dark night was approching, the wind at N. E. and the storm unabated; however, we did not abandon ourselves to dispair, but succeeded in getting the mainsail tolerably well set, and by lying in the hollow of the sea, the ship got head way. At day light in the morning, we were abreast of Dimlington, and about three miles off. Humber was now our only hope, which if we missed, we must (as the wind was) in a few hours have inevitably perished.

We made every effort in our power to get the

ship to veer; as the lee fore-topsail-brace was broke, we got a warp from the main mast head, to the said yard arm; got the tattered sail to fill; and, with the help of the sprit-sail, got her off from the wind; then steering for the Spurn Point, we crossed the Newcome in broken water, but did not touch. As the ship steered very wide, we got both main tacks to the chess trees; and as the wind was too scant to get into the Hawke, and having a strong ebb tide, we let go our anchor a little above the Spurn Point; then letting go the main-geers, the main yard came down; for we were so exhausted by hunger and fatigue we could not haul the main-sail up. Two or three days after we got up to Whitebooth Road, from whence we were driven by ice, and forced to sea with a contrary wind.

In the spring of 1769, I sailed on a voyage to Memel. On arriving off that place with several other ships, pilots came on board. I had been there the year before; and when I left the place there was 14 to 15 feet on the bar; but during winter the ice, brought down by the current, instead of driving out to sea had lodged on the bar; so that now there was only eight or nine feet of water. The pilots who knew this, did not acquaint us with the circumstance, but ran several of us on the bar, where we lay striking on the ground, and against each other, until our ship, and one belonging to John Hurry, were wrecked. A few got in, but several throwing athwart before they came to the shoalest part, drove out to sea. The reason given by the pilots was a very cruel one, namely, that if they had acquainted us with the true state of the bar, we should have gone to Riga. No doubt they were instructed by the Memel merchants, who were known to be unprincipled men!

In the winter of 1770, I was master of the Joseph, belonging to Benjamin Chapman, on a passage from Shields to London; we came to anchor in Yarmouth, or rather Corton-road as did several other ships; at which time there was little or no appearance of storm. I had laid down to sleep; it was low water in the evening; but was soon awoke by the violent shaking of the mizen stay-sail, which had been used in swinging the ship. I turned out immediately, went on deck, and seeing a dismal looking sky, in the N. and N. N. E. and the wind changed to that quarter, I knocked all hands out, got the sheet anchor clear, let it go, and bore away both cables to near the ends. By thus bearing away before the whole weight of the gale fell upon us, our anchors providentially did not start; but before we got the cables served, the gale came on so heavy that the people were washed from the hause. During the night, a brig parted, and drove towards us, with our masts in one; she fell upon our cables, but they grew out so far and were so tight, that she was thereby thrown off; but left part of her jib on our bowsprit-end. Another ship cast with her head in, and came stern foremast against our larboard bow, but did us no injury.

At day light in the morning, we found few ships that had rode out the gale. Many were wrecked on Corton-sand, and on the Holmhead we saw several wrecks. This was indeed an afflicting sight!

One ship in particular[*] lay near the north-end of Corton-sand; the whole crew got into the shrouds of one of the masts, which we saw

---

[*] The Thomas, of Newcastle, John Ash, master.

fall and they all perished! She lay so far to windward that it was impossible for us to help them; but a Sunderland brig, called the Chance, lay near abreast of us, and seemed not likely to break up soon. I was extremely distressed at the sight, but durst not propose our attempting to save them. The people saw my anxiety, and anticipated my wishes. My mate*, a bold and smart young man, and four apprentices who had been Sunderland keelmen, generously offered to try to save the poor distressed seamen. I gave them leave to make the attempt, charging them, that when they came near the wreck, if they found the boat in danger of swamping, that they should be sure to return. We had, however, the pleasure to see them get under the ship's lee, where the sea was tolerably smooth, and we had also the additional pleasure to see them returning with nine men and boys. There were other nine left on board; for a vessel called the Spirit Brig had drove foul of the Chance, the crew of which had got on board her. My heroic mate

* Robert Dixon, who lives at North Shields at the time of printing these memoirs.

and lads would go again, and try to bring off the remainder, in which they succeeded; and thus saved seventeen, which but for them would soon have found a watery grave! (One of the last nine being dead when they brought him on board). The said seventeen were, I believe, all that were saved out of the many ships lost in this dreadful storm. No boats could get off from Yarmouth to assist the suffering seamen.

How valuable and how useful is true courage, when exerted in the cause of humanity! To save others at the risk of our own lives (from disinterested motives) argues true nobility of mind.

If, as history records, the ancient Romans decreed a civic crown to that man who saved the life of one citizen, what reward was not due to these five young men, who, at the imminent risk of their own lives, saved seventeen? But they received no reward whatever, either from the public, or from those most interested.

It should be impressed on the minds of boys, on their first going to sea, that a strict and prompt obedience to command is so necessary a duty, that if they never know how to obey, they will never know how, nor be fit to command; that nothing but a strict discipline, and a generous contempt of danger, will make them good seamen.

To preserve order in a ship, the master should observe a dignified conduct; and in all things set a good example. He should never command his men to do any unnecessary work; and he should avoid too much familiarity with them. His mate should be his companion and confidant, in whom if he sees any occasion for reproof, he should take care that he never do it in the hearing of his men or boys, as that would bring him into contempt, and lessen his authority.

The mate, also, should observe a prudent reserve with regard to his intercourse with the sailors; remembering the old adage, that "Too much familiarity breeds contempt."

There is another duty incumbent on both master and mate, which is that of keeping a good look out during night, to prevent those fatal accidents which too often happen at sea, from neglect of this necessary duty. They should not suffer the men in their respective watches to lounge on the windlass or hatch-comings; but oblige two of them to keep a good look out, and mind that they answer the call: But thoughtful masters and mates will not wholly depend on them, but will frequently look under the foot, and to leeward of the leach of the foresail.

This is the more necessary as sailors, not having much weight of care on their minds, are too often inattentive, and sometimes fall asleep when they ought to be awake.

Another necessary duty, especially on this coast, is that of frequently casting the lead. Suppose on your passage from London, you leave Cromer with a S. E. wind, and thick or hazy weather, as you draw towards the Head, do not come within 18 fathoms water; you will know when you have passed the Head by falling into deeper water; if then the thick weather continue, the wind at S. E. or E. S. E. and likely to blow strong, do not steer along shore in hope of gaining your port, but set down your tacks, and get such an offing that you will be in no danger of driving a shore. What dreadful losses have I known to have happened from too eager a desire to get into port! Even in crossing the North Sea it is necessary to have recourse to the lead.

I remember a case in point. A number of us bound to the Baltic, crossed the sea at the same time. It is particularly necessary to sound the Jut's Reef, in order to know by the depth of the water your distance from the Norway land, also whether to the northward or southward of the right line of course.

There were in company two of the most experienced Baltic traders belonging to Whitby, Captains Benson and Shafto. These men depended so much on their knowledge as to neglect sounding the Jut's Reef, and found themselves unexpectedly on the rocks before morning, whilst the rest in company, with less knowledge, but more prudence, ran clear.

Crossing the North Sea from the westward, ships are generally a-head of their reckoning, and the contrary in coming from the eastward. A strong current generally sets to the northward near the Norway coast, especially if the wind is in the S. W. quarter, for which allowance should be made.

In the thirty-fifth year of my age, at the pressing importunity of my wife and friends, I left the sea, and settled on shore in the business of ship and insurance broker, in North

Shields. I have often on a comparison between a life of business on shore, and a sea-faring one, given the latter the preference; and with the knowledge I have of both situations, if I had my time to begin again, I would be a sailor. I know that a very great majority (especially of religious people) are against me, but very few of that majority are capable of making a true estimate; having knowledge only of one side of the question: the general objections of landsmen to a sea-faring life are dangers—corruption of morals—and hardships.

Dangers at sea are certainly more apparent than on land, but whether really so or not, is a question to be solved by those who are skilled in computing deaths and population. There are probably as many seamen who attain old age (in proportion to their number) as there are manufacturers, miners, men in various sedentary employments, and such as waste their lives in regular sensuality. The naturally timerous may stay on land, and the wicked should repent and fear Him who rules on sea as well as on dry land.

When the mind has got a right bias, a sea-faring life is favourable to a religious growth;

the ancients thought so, when they said, " If a man would learn to pray let him go to sea;" and from what the Psalmist says on the subject, it is evident he thought " Going down to the sea in ships, occupying business on the waters, and seeing the wonders of the Lord in the great deep," were likely means to excite in the mind prayer for protection and praise for deliverance.

But it may be said, whatever effect a seafaring life had on the ancients, we see evident proofs that seamen are more wicked than other men. I acknowledge that the generality of seamen are wicked; they may be apparently more so than others, but not so in reality. I have thought much on the subject, and give it as my opinion, that if seamen had the same labour bestowed on them that is on landsmen, they would as much exceed them in a reverential awe of the Almighty as they now do in generosity and humanity!

As to hardships, they are almost entirely ideal, if we may judge from the lively disposition of sailors. The hardships they suffer do not affect their spirits, for they often sleep on a wet deck, or on a hard chest-lid, go to their beds with wet cloaths, and turn out to take their four hours watch, without receiving the least injury.

It must be acknowledged, that seaman have often to endure long watchings, and great fatigue in cold and rainy weather, but this serves only to give them a higher relish for ease and sleep than it is possible for those to know whose lives are one continued sameness.

A life of regular sensuality, as well as a more vicious conduct, enfeebles the mind and stagnates the spirits. The food they eat turns to wind, and fills their heads with melancholic vapors. I have sometimes seen people as much dread getting their feet wet, or, when in the house, to have a little air blow upon them through a crack in the window, or a crevice in the door, as a sailor feels when a blast of wind carries all the masts by the board.

The highest degree of human happiness is not always the portion of the affluent, who eat and drink and sleep, when and where they please. Gratification of any kind palls the appetite, and a continued sameness of indulgence creates disgust. A chequered life is the best and safest; it makes men thankful for prosperity when they are favoured with it, and when by too much indulgence they are nearly lulled asleep, dangers and personal hardships rouse, and more loud than a human voice tells them, "This is not their rest."

In November, 1766, I married a virtuous young woman, in the methodist connection. She was with me in the dreadful new year's gale, already mentioned; and although no attention could be paid to her, and a considerable quantity of water was in the cabin, she shewed no signs of fear on her own account; her only fear was that I should be washed over board.

In 1778, I united in society with the people called Quakers: my wife had been taken into membership two years before, and, to the time of her death, which happened in 1794, was much respected by Friends.

In a commercial country, like Great Britain, particular attention should be paid to render the navigation on its coasts as safe as possible. There are few so dangerous as the East coast of this kingdom. Sand banks lie a considerable distance from, and others out of sight of land. From the Spurn to the Thames, the channel is between sand banks and the main, and frequently between one sand bank and another.

But the greatest danger to which ships bound from the northern and eastern ports to London were exposed, was owing to the want of light to guide them either into Yarmouth Roads, or through Hasboro' Gatt. This channel, though often made use of with day-light, was seldom (and then only with extreme hazard) attempted during night.

There appeared to many well-informed mariners a want of more lights; and about this time there was a project for lighting the Cockle-gatt, but it fell to the ground. The few lights at that time were very bad: I have often known ships lay-to, and fire guns, to awaken the drowsy attenders, and oblige them to stir up their fires!

Many years after I first went to sea, I have been in ships obliged to lay-to at noon, off the Dodgeon, with strong northerly winds and high sea, because it was impossible in a short winter's day, to save day-light into Yarmouth Roads: there we lay under no command, and in continual danger of driving foul of each other. These were distressing times!

Towards midnight we would have bore away, but were afraid of falling on the north end of Hasboro' Sand, or on Sheringham Shoal, because we could not depend on seeing Cromer light, it was so bad that it seldom could be seen so far to the eastward as the former, or so far to the northward as the latter; on this account it not unfrequently happened that even the next day we could not save day-light into Yarmouth Roads, nor out of Hasboro' Gatt, and were obliged to bring up under Winterton, a very hazardous situation.

There must have been unpardonable neglect in the corporation of the Trinity-house Deptford Strond, to suffer the trade to be so much exposed. They are, as we are told, conservators of the coast; but it is evident they have suffered the lights on the coast so long to remain bad, that it became proverbial with sailors to say, " As bad as Cromer and Orfordness lights." They might have done many things for the preservation of shipping, and the lives of seamen, with the revenue they have been in receipt of, which is so great, that only themselves know how great it is; for they never have, and I believe never intend, to account for the distribution of it. They seem to be privileged above every other corporation, though all other corporations are injurious to the public. This is strikingly exemplified in the two cases of the Tyne and the Wear: the former are in the receipt of a considerable revenue for the purpose of mending the port of Shields and the river Tyne; but a very small part, or rather no part at all, of this revenue is applied to the intended purpose, so that the port and river grows worse and worse every year. In many parts where large ships floated at low water, there is not more than five or six feet.

At Sunderland, where commissioners are appointed by a particular act of parliament, with a very small tax on shipping, they have done astonishing things: they have turned the course of the river, they have torn up rocks from the bottom of it; and have built extensive and expensive piers, so that now there is fourteen or fifteen feet on the bar, where formerly there was not more than five or six.

The corporation of Newcastle are indeed subject to, and often called on by the burgesses to an account, but that is chiefly about their own privileges—not how they dispose of the revenue for those just and general purposes for which they are paid by the shipping interest.

As hinted before, there was a great want of more lights on the coast, and of mending those that were established; the neglect of doing which drew down great responsibility on those whose proper business it was to remedy the evil.

I had used the sea twenty-two years, twelve of which I commanded ships mostly in the coal trade, that best nursery for seamen; and since the year 1772, had been employed on shore as ship and insurance broker. During this time having occasion to adjust many averages and losses, the hardships and sufferings of seamen, the means of alleviating them, and of preventing the loss of so many valuable lives, became subjects of deep consideration with me. There happened at this period an event which more than ordinary afflicted me: it was that tremendous storm which happened between the thirty-first of October, and the first of November, 1789, when twenty-three ships were lost on the Norfolk coast, and about three hundred seamen perished!

This dreadful event awakened the attention of the ship owners in the north, to the consideration of means to prevent the like calamity in future.

At this momentous time I produced a plan for making Hasboro' Gatt a safe night passage, by placing two leading lights near Hasboro' church, and a floating light at the north-end of the New-arp-sand, with three lanterns, so that ships from the eastward might not mistake it for the Dodgeon: which scheme I laid before five or six of the most intelligent seamen, my neighbours, and which they very highly approved. But considering the diversity of opinions that prevailed in Shields, I thought it best to consult seamen at other ports, and get their opinion, before I made it further known amongst my neighbours. In this my most sanguine expectations were exceeded: I received letters from Stockton, Whitby, Scarborough, Hull, and London, fully approving the plan, without suggesting any alteration; at the same time promising to unite in applications to the Trinity-house for the immediate execution of it. (See the appendix). When these letters were shewn to the ship-owners of the port of Newcastle, all soon united in an application for the Gatt being lighted, conformable to the said plan, which was carried into effect in the autumn of 1790; and the most beneficial consequences have resulted therefrom. Few if any ships have been lost there since; and it is now found to be a wide, clear, and safe night passage, such as I had described it to be.

On a retrospect of the heavy losses that have happened to commerce, generally, and the lives of seamen, in the last sixty years, when the first proposition for placing this light is stated to have been made to, or by the Trinity-board (as the present board told R. Burdon, Esq. and myself) one cannot but query, Why did not the board at that time survey the Gatt? Had they done so, they would, doubtless, have found it to be the same clear channel it is now proved to be. I had known it to be frequented above forty years, whenever with northerly winds sight could be got of Hasboro' church, so as to bring it to bear about W. N. W. but then such was the dread of the Newarp-sand, that ships usually ran twice the necessary distance before they durst haul to the southward. This inconvenience was still preferable to risking a long winter's night at anchor, under Winterton; or laying-to under sail until day light, as already mentioned; the consequences of which are fully described in the appendix, No. 6.

Encouraged by the success of the plan for lighting Hasboro' Gatt, I conceived that similar improvements might be made in other parts of the coast; and it occurred to me, that a floating light at the north end of the Goodwin Sands would be of very great utility.

I no sooner communicated this idea, (which I did in the year 1791) than the trade adopted it; and the ports of Newcastle, Sunderland, Scarborough, Burlington, Hull, and Liverpool, petitioned the Trinity-house to place the said light, without loss of time.

On an intimation from the board that they would not comply with the request of the memorialists, unless the port of London united in it; the ship-owners in the port of Newcastle addressed those of London, stating the benefits that would accrue to the trade in general, by a light so situated; and giving proofs from their own knowledge of the losses that had happened from the want of such a light; and describing the gross impositions practised on suffering seamen by the boatmen of Broadstairs, Ramsgate, and Deal. (See No. 9.)

This address being sent to an eminent merchant in London*, he got it printed, and put into the hands of those most interested in shipping and commerce; in consequence of which, about the middle of 1792, a meeting was held at the London Tavern, when the plan for a floating light was unanimously approved, and a memorial presented to the Trinity-board, which induced them to consent to the measure, after having corrected the petitions in the manner shewn in No. 10, by which their idea of its utility will fully appear. (See also their letter to George Denholm, No. 14.)

Nothing can more fully demonstrate their sense of the importance of the lights in Hasboro' Gatt, than this letter; for, had not the Gatt been lighted, the *hundred sail* mentioned in that letter must have anchored under Winterton; and as the wind was then northerly (the most dangerous wind on the Norfolk coast) many of them, probably, would have been lost before morning.

* A. Brough, Esq.

In this letter of the Trinity-board's there are circumstances worthy of notice. The danger to which these ships were exposed is much exaggerated; and there seems no small misapprehension in the following declaration:

" That the greatest concern which the corporation, as well as the ship-owners, must and ought to feel on this occasion, is the risk navigation has been exposed to, during the time the lights could not be exhibited;" because, in fact, they were not exposed to danger from the want of the Floating-light; the leading lights guide safely through, independent of the Float, when the night is so clear that they can be seen at a considerable distance, as the night of the twenty-third of February, 1791, is stated to have been: and the *hundred sail* having passed safely through, is a corroborating proof, that the danger to which they were exposed was not great. The only inconvenience they suffered was that of running further to the eastward than they needed to have done, had not the light been driven from her moorings. Here the leading lights appear to great advantage; indeed without them it would have been unsafe to have entered the Gatt, especially in showery weather, when ships often run more than half through, before they get sight of the Float.

It also often happens in stormy weather, that the lights are alternately obscured and discovered; so that ships have two guides, one ahead, and the other astern of them. It must be a great relief to the anxious mariner to find, that, when one light is enveloped in thick darkness, the other is distinctly seen.

About a month previous to the meeting at the London Tavern, I was desired to go to London, to solicit the Board to place the light at the Goodwin; and to request of them, as a compensation, a lease of it for a few years. It had been proposed by the ship-owners in the north to reward me by a subscription; but this did not accord with my feelings, as it would fall partially. I wished, if any compensation was to be made me, that it might be made more general; and no mode appeared to me so agreeable as to be put in possession of a lease of the light, to which I would have taken a pleasure in attending, and in making it as useful as possible. I accordingly petitioned the Board, (see No. 8.) which petition was handed to the master of the Trinity-house (William Pitt), and by him given to the deputy-master.

R. Burdon, Esq. M. P. went with me to the Trinity-house, to speak to the Board on my behalf: but before we got there the Board had separated, and only the secretary remained; with him some conversation ensued on the business which carried us there. He appeared very polite, and promised, on the member's account, to introduce me to the Board; at the same time assured us, that they had determined to let no more leases, giving, as a reason, that the lights in private hands were badly kept. This reason would appear just to any but a seaman; and I believe the said member felt the full force of it. I knew that the lights in private hands were not worse kept than those under the care of the Board; and was not willing that my friend should go away under wrong impressions: I, therefore, asked the secretary if Cromer-light did not belong to them? On his answering in the affirmative, I replied, " That there was not a worse light on all the coast;" that it often could not be seen at the distance of three miles; that it had been in that state ever since I could remember; and, that owing to its badness, many ships had been lost on Sheringham Shoal, and the north-end of Hasboro' Sand.

On the next Board-day another member of parliament* attended with me on my behalf, but without effect. The Board told him, that the light vessel could not ride in so exposed a situation, but would break adrift and drown all the people; and further, that if a lease was granted, the expense of maintaining it would be so great, so as to leave no profit! Impressed with these ideas, the said M. P. advised me to give it up, and look for a compensation from some other quarter.

Was it not mean in the Trinity-board to impose on the said gentleman, by impressing his mind with needless fears? They knew at the time, that what they told him was not at all likely to happen; for they could not but know that the Dodgeon and Newarp lights rode safely, in situations at least as much exposed.

I was now called before the Board; but, as I was going through the lobby, the secretary

* Wm. Wilberforce, Esq.

took me aside, and said, " Mr Taylor, you were not the original projector of the lights in Hasboro' Gatt;" and read part of a letter, said to have been sent by one of the brethren to a ship-owner at Shields, prior to my plan reaching London. I said no more to him than that of such letter I had never heard before.

On appearing before the Board, which seemed to be a very full one, I was asked, by the deputy-master, upon what I grounded my claim of a lease of the Goodwin-light? I answered, on the documents I held in my hand, (which were most of these I now publish) but added, " That your secretary has just read to me the copy of a letter, said to be written by a member of this house, who may be present for aught I know; that, of such a letter I had never heard before; and, although I could not say that it was never written, I could venture to say, that such a letter never reached Shields: for it was not at all probable, that a letter on such a subject, at such a time, should have reached Shields, and I not have heard of it!"

The questions asked by the deputy-master were very frivolous; and in conclusion, he said, " We acknowledge your merits; but having resolved to let no more leases, we cannot let you have a lease of the Goodwin-light;" and added, " You had better go home, and stay no longer in London on expenses." See, in this deputy, the insolence of office! I had not tasted a morsel of bread, nor one glass of wine, at the Board's expense; and yet I was advised to go home to save my own expenses! At this time I had been at many hundred pounds expense, and the Board was in the annual receipt of many thousands from the tax on the lights planned and matured by me!

I returned home soon after this interview; and on my arrival at Shields, to my great surprise found, that, during my absence, an elder brother of the Trinity-house had sent down to a particular friend the newspaper called the Public Ledger, of the third of December, 1789, in which was an essay, recommending to the ship-owners of the port of Newcastle, to apply to the Trinity-house for lights in Hasboro' Gatt. The essay was dated North Shields 27th of November, and signed an " *Old Seaman*;" but on applying to the person to whom the said paper was sent, for a sight of it, I saw that the initials of one of the elder brethren were penciled on it; and when I shewed him a copy of my first letter to Thomas Hall, dated the 21st of November, and his answer to me, dated the 27th of same month (see No. 1.) and saw that the essay was partly a transcript of my said letter, he exclaimed, " I am ashamed of Mr——" The plan was sent to the Trinity-house, Scarborough, on the 18th, as appears by a letter from thence, dated the 22d (see No. 2.) it was at Hull and Whitby the 27th. (See No. 4. John Chapman's letter.)

The design of sending the essay down to Shields in my absence, was to persuade the ship-owners that the said essay was that which first called their attention to the lights in Hasboro' Gatt; as three years had elapsed since the lights were applied for; and, as the reader will find, I did not immediately make my plan public at Shields, and no such paper as the Public Ledger being taken in there, some ship-owners doubted whether it might not have been so; but they certified that they had never seen the essay in question. (See No. 5.) It happened unluckily for the writer of the essay, that it was dated as from Shields on the twenty-seventh of November, and was inserted in the Ledger of third of December and could not reach Shields before the fifth of that month; whereas my plan, as before stated, was in London on the fourth of November, and shown to the Trinity-board!

I had observed, when I first saw the Public Ledger, that the stroke of a pen had been put through the 2 to make it 17, instead of 27, that it might seem to be before the date of my first letter to Thomas Hall. Being in London some years after, I desired a friend of mine to take me to a coffee-house, that filed public papers; for I thought, that from what was done to the Public Ledger sent to Shields, some of the Board might have gone to the different coffee-houses and made the same alteration. We accordingly went to Peel's coffee-house, and on looking at the Public Ledger of the third of December, 1789, we found, as I expected, the two made into one! We called the waiter, and asked him, what that figure was? He answered, " It was a two, but you see it is made one!" We asked, who made it so? He said he did not know. It ought not to be supposed that many members of the Trinity-House were in the secret of this attempt of one of their brethren, to arrogate to himself the merit of lighting Hasboro' Gatt, but it is evident that some of them were; and that they continued to propogate such a falsehood for a considerable time after, notwithstanding the written evidence adduced (see No. 5.), signed by most of the principal ship-owners, and would have been signed by all, if it had been thought necessary.

The conduct of a part of the Trinity-board can be accounted for on no other principle, but that they thought it a reflection on them, that an obscure individual should be the author of schemes for improving navigation of such acknowledged public utility; and to which if proper attention had been paid by those whose particular business it was, thousands of lives, and millions of property, might have been saved to this country. (See No. 6.)

Notwithstanding the powerful memorials to the Board, and their promise to comply with the memorialist's request, little or nothing further was heard of it for about two years. Grieved at this procrastination, for which no reason could be assigned, I took the liberty to rouse the attention of the board, by a letter, dated the twenty-ninth of September, 1794, which I got printed and sent to the different merchants, and coffee-houses in London, (No. 7.) I had soon afterwards the pleasure to see in the public prints, the intention of the Board to place the light, which was done soon afterwards.

It will be seen by the following advertisement, that no ship grounded on the Goodwin during the winter in which the light was placed, although the winds had been uncommonly tempestuous, whereas from the twelfth to the twenty-seventh of November, 1794, five sail were wrecked there and many of the crews perished. (See No. 7.) The advertisement appeared in the Sun newspaper, on the fifth of January, 1796.

" The Master of the Trinity-house has removed the floating light which was moored near the North-head of the Goodwin, a quarter of a mile nearer the English land: it has already proved its usefulness, as not one vessel of any description has grounded on that part, since the light was placed there the twenty-fourth of August last."

I had also the satisfaction to find that Cromer light was made a very good one. This light cannot be of any use to navigation, unless it can be seen as far off as the north-end of Hasboro'-sand, and as far to the northward as Sheringham-shoal; but (as hinted before, in a conversation with the secretary of the Trinity-house) it often could not be seen one third of that distance. Is it not then more than probable that many of the losses on Hasboro' and Sheringham have been owing to the badness of this light?

Orfordness and the North-Foreland lights were also very bad ones; and Winterton was little better; but since by placing lights near Hasboro'-church, the latter has not only become unnecessary, but a real nuisance. It seems to have been mended at the very time it should have been taken away, and the trade eased of the burthen of maintaining it, as requested by the ship owners in their memorials to the Trinity-house.

I had observed, with no small concern the damage frequently sustained by ships in the Downs, and was convinced that it was chiefly occasioned by the masters and mates of ships using the West India, Mediterranean, and other Southern trades, not knowing as they ought to do that necessary branch of seamanship, the art of managing a ship at single anchor. I also knew that very few such accidents happened to colliers. I have known upwards of one hundred sail lie wind-bound in Yarmouth-roads two or three weeks in perfect safety; nor do I remember, in the two-and-twenty years that I used the sea, ever to have seen a foul anchor hove up in a road-stead; but, although colliers ride easy near each other, that is not the case when what they call a South Spainer brings up near them; and they usually take the first opportunity of removing to a considerable distance from such a one.

In 1792, I published instructions for managing ships at single anchor, which I simplified as much as possible, that the whole might be re-retained in memory. I submitted these instructions to the examination of the mariners of North Shields, (than whom, none understand the subject better); they at a public meeting, came to the following resolution, and ordered it to be entered in their books:

" That it is the opinion of this meeting, that many of the losses that happen at sea, are owing to the cuases mentioned in the preface to H.

Taylor's instructions to young mariners; which instructions we approve, and recommend to the attention of every description of seamen; and that a number of the said instructions be purchased and put on board each of our ships."

I received the following official letters from the Trinity-houses of London and Hull, promising to promote the circulation of this tract; indeed, it would be well if they made a point of doing it; for there is too much reason to fear that few of the pilots, except those bred in the coal trade, know how to manage ships at single anchor. I do not know whether the subject makes a part of the examination of pilots; if it does not, I think it ought.

*Trinity House, London, Sept.*1, 1792.

" I have communicated to the brethren of
" the corporation your letter of the 8th past,
" relating to your publication of instructions
" to mariners, respecting the management of
" ships at single anchor; and have to acquaint
" you, that a number of them have been purchas-
" ed and perused, and being approved of by
" the brethren, they have recommended them

" to the attention of such young mariners as
" they are acquainted with.

"I am, &c.

DAVID COURT."

" Henry Taylor,
" North Shields.

Trinity House, Hull, Sept. 1, 1792.

" Sir,
" I have the command of this corporation to
" acquaint you, in answer to your letter of the
" 6th ulto. that the Board approve much of
" your instructions for the management of
" ships at single anchor; and will recommend
" the use of them to the shipping of this port.
" You will therefore think it right to send a
" number of them to some bookseller in this
" place.

" I am, &c.
" ROBERT GREEN, SEC."

" Henry Taylor,
" North Shields.

The following are the instructions alluded to; and, as nothing of the same principle has been published, I do not hesitate to give them a place here.

ON THE MANAGEMENT OF SHIPS AT SINGLE ANCHOR.

Riding in a tide-way, with a fresh of wind, the ship should have what is called a short or windward service, about forty-five fathoms of cable, and always sheered to windward*, not

---

* It has been thought by some theorists, that ships should be sheered to leeward of their anchor; but the common practice of the most experienced seamen is against that opinion; for it is found that when a ship rides leeward-tide and sheered to windward, with the wind two or three points upon the bow, and blowing hard, in the interval between the squalls the sheer will draw her towards the wind's eye; so that when the next squall comes, before she be pressed a-stream of her anchor, it is probable that there will be a lull again, and the spring which the cable got by the sheer, will greatly ease it during the squall.

Riding with the wind two or three points upon the quarter, when the wind and tide are nearly of equal strength, and when ships are so liable to break their sheer, if the helm should be a-weather, or the ship sheered to leeward, I cannot conceive how she can do otherwise than be continually breaking her sheer.

Every seaman knows that no ship without a rudder, or with the helm left loose, will veer; they always in such situations fly to: this proves that with the wind pressing upon the quarter, and the helm a-lee, a ship will be less liable to break her sheer, than when the helm is a-weather. Besides if the helm is a-lee when she breaks her sheer, it will be a-weather when the wind comes on the other quarter, as it ought to be until she either swing to leeward, or coming to a sheer the other way, bring the buoy on the lee-quarter. Now if a ship break her sheer with the helm a-weather, it throws her head to the wind so suddenly, as scarce to give time to brace the yards about, and very probably she will fall over her anchor before the fore-stay-sail can be got up.

always with the helm hard down but more or less so, according to the strength or weakness of the tide; ships have often been known to sheer their anchor home, drive on board of other ships, and on the sands near them, before it was discovered that the anchor had been removed from the place where it was let go.

WHEN THE SHIP WILL BACK.

When the wind is cross, or nearly cross, off shore, or in the opposite direction, ships will always back; this is done by the mizen-topsail, assisted if needful by the mizen-staysail, such as have no mizen-topsail, commonly use the main top-sail, or if it blow fresh a top-gallant-sail, or any such sail, at the gaff.

In backing, a ship should always wend with a tawt cable, that you may be sure the anchor is drawn round; in case their is not a sufficiency of wind for that purpose, the ship should be hove a-peak.

HOW THE YARDS OUGHT TO BE BRACED.

Riding with the wind afore the beam, the yards should be braced forward: if a-baft the beam, brace them all a-back.

RIDING WINDWARD TIDE IN DANGER OF BREAKING HER SHEER.

If the wind be so far aft that a ship will not back, (which should never be attempted, if when the tide eases, she forge a-head, and bring the buoy on the lee quarter) she should be set a head; if the wind be far aft, and blowing fresh, the utmost care and attention is necessary, as ships riding in this situation often break their sheer and come to windward of their anchors again. When a ship lies in this ticklish situation, the after yards must be braced forward, and the head yards the contrary way; she will lay safe as long as the buoy continues on the larboard quarter. With the helm thus, and the wind right aft, or nearly so, the starboard, main, and fore braces should be hauled in: this supposes the main braces to lead forward.

TENDING TO LEEWARD, WHEN THE SHIP MUST BE SET A-HEAD.

When a ship begins to tend to leeward, and the buoy comes on the weather quarter, the first thing to be done is to brace about the head yards; and when the wind comes near the beam, set the foretopmast staysail* and keep it standing until it shake; then brace all the yards sharp forward, especially if it be likely to blow strong.

HOW TO MANAGE WHEN THE SHIP BREAKS HER SHEER.

If laying in the aforesaid position, and she break her sheer, brace ab ut the main yard immediately; if she recover and bring the buoy on the lee or larboard quarter, let the after-yards be again braced about; but if she come to a sheer the other way, by bringing the buoy on the other quarter, change the helm and brace the head-yards to.

WHEN A LONG SERVICE IS OUT, AND THE SHIP IS LIKELY TO GO TO WINDWARD.

Riding leeward tide with more cable than the windward service, and expecting the ship will go to windward of her anchor, begin as soon as the tide eases to shorten in the cable.

---

* It sometimes happens that when the fore stay-sail is set too soon the ship's head will pay round off, and she will break her sheer; to prevent this, and to keep the wind broad upon the beam, it will often e found necessary to set the mizen stay sail also; which should always be hauled down as soon as the wind comes before the beam, otherwise the ship s head will be thrown in the wind too soon.

This is often hard work, but it is necessary to be done, otherwise the anchor may be fouled by the great length of cable the ship has to draw round; but even if this could be done without fouling the anchor, the cable would be damaged against the bows, or cut-water. Observe, that when a ship rides windward tide, the cable should be cackled from the short service towards the anchor, as far as will prevent the bare part touching the ship.

When the ship tends to windward and must be set a-head, hoist the fore-stay-sail as soon as it will stand*, and when the buoy comes on the lee-quarter haul down the fore-topmast-staysail, brace to the head yards, and put the helm a lee; for till then the helm must be kept a-weather, and all the yards full.

HOW TO MANAGE IN A STORM.

When a ship rides leeward-tide, and the wind increases, care should be taken to give her more cable in time; otherwise the anchor may start, and she may not easily be brought up again, and this care is the more necessary, when she rides in the hause of any ship. Pre-

---

* In moderate weather the jib may also be set.

viously to giving a long service, it is usual to take a weather-bit, that is, a turn of the cable over the windlass-end, that in bearing away, the ship may not overpower you. Grease the service, for that will prevent its chafing in the hause*.

If the gale continue to increase, the topmast should be timely struck, but the fore-yard should seldom if ever be lowered down, that in case of parting, the foresail may always be ready. At such time, there should be more men on deck than the common anchor watch†, that no accident may happen from inattention, or falling asleep.

In a tide-way a second anchor should never be let go, but when absolutuly necessary; a ship will sometimes ride easier and safer, (especially if the sea run high) with a very long scope of cable, and one anchor, than with less length and two anchors: however, it is adviseable, as a preventative, when ships have not

---

* Every ship should have two or more leather services.

† The common anchor-watch, in colliers, consists of two, an experienced man and a boy. It is thus that boys are early taught their duty: and it was formerly thought a great honor for a young man, during his apprenticeship, to have the charge of an anchor-watch.

room to drive, and the night is dark, to let fall a second anchor under foot, with a range of cable along the deck: if this be not thought necessary, the deep sea lead should be thrown over-board, and the line frequently handled by the watch, that they may be assured she rides fast.

CAUTION RESPECTING THE ANCHOR WATCH.

If at any time the anchor-watch, presuming on their own knowledge, should wend the ship, or suffer her to break her sheer without calling the mate, he should immediately, or the very first opportunity, oblige the crew to heave the anchor in sight; which will prevent the commission of the like fault again: for besides the share of trouble the watch will have, the rest of the crew will blame them for neglecting their duty.

PARTICULAR DUTY OF THE CHIEF MATE.

Prudent mates seldom lay a week in a roadstead without heaving their anchor in sight; even though they have not the least suspicion of its being foul. There are other reasons why the anchor should be looked at: sometimes the cable receives damage by sweeping wrecks, or anchors, that have been lost; or from rocks, or stones, and it is often necessary to trip the anchor, in order to take a clearer birth; which should be done as often as any ship brings up too near. Do not spend time disputing with those who may have given you a foul birth, for while you are so doing the wind may increase and prevent you shifting your situation, and the most fatal consequences may follow from your riding too near other ships; for one ship badly situated with respect to others, with bad ground tackling, and worse management, may be the means of driving twenty sail adrift on the strand, or sands near them.

A good road-stead is better and safer than a bad harbour; therefore never leave the former for the latter, but in case of real necessity; and I know but of one case where it can be necessary, and that is, when you can ride no longer and have no lee-road to fly to for refuge.

No ship, however strong or fully built, can lay a-ground loaden, without receiving damage, and probably a great deal more than at first discovers itself. Sharp-built ships in such situations often break their bottom timbers: this they may do and yet swim; but coming to work at sea, the hidden wounds often break out, and inevitable ruin follows. Some of them, however, fortunately for their crews, receive so much damage as to be condemned in the harbour.

It seldom happens but ships have an opportunity of changing their road-steads; as, with a northerly wind, from Yarmouth Roads to Leostoff South-road; and with the wind to the eastward of north, from thence to Osley Bay. There are many instances of colliers that have gone seven years, eight or ten voyages each year, and never in all that time put into harbour by the way.

Ships waiting in the Downs for a wind to go westward, should, when it begins to blow southerly, and the sea makes, take their anchors up, and go to Margate Road; especially such as ride to leeward, and are exposed to the danger of others driving foul of them. The trouble of frequently looking at the anchor, or changing a road-stead, should never be an object of consideration; but rather consider that on so doing may depend the safety of the ship, and cargo, and even of your lives.

As chief-mates are known to have the charge

of ships at anchor, it behoves them to be very attentive to this part of their duty. Heaving the anchor a-peak, or the anchor in sight, shifting a birth, or changing a road-stead, may often cause the sailors to grumble; but that should not prevent mates from the execution of their duty, nor raise any thing vindictive in their minds so as to dispose them to treat them ill, or give them a great deal of unnecessary trouble. This is a disposition, the indulgence of which will procure them the contempt of every generous seaman; for it is a general maxim, that the man who uses a seaman ill, is no seaman himself. There may be exceptions to this general rule, but they are very few.

I received two letters on the subject of the lights, of which the following are copies.

Harley Street, 19 *May*, 1792.

" I have examined two papers produced to
" me by Henry Taylor, of North Shields, in
" which the committees of the ports of New-
" castle and Sunderland acknowledge him to be

" the author of Hasboro'-lights; and I know
" the signatures to be those of the persons
" most conversant, and interested in the trade
" of those ports.

" ROWLAND BURDON."

" Henry Taylor,
 " North Shields.

London, 24 May, 1792.

" I have looked over the greatest part of
" your papers, and they so well convince me
" of your merits with the public, that I shall be
" glad to render you any service I am able, in
" obtaining for you the remuneration to which
" you are intitled. I shall confer with Mr
" Burdon on the subject.

" WM. WILBERFORCE."

" Henry Taylor,
 " North Shields.

The following testimonials also relate to the same subject; the numbers of which have been referred to in the preceding part of the memoirs.

(No. 1,)

London, November 27, 1789,
No. 22, *Jewry Street.*

" Dear Sir,

" I have received your letter of the 21st
" instant, and have duly considered the plan
" and observations you have made, on the in-
" tended erection of new light-houses near
" Hasboro', and a floating light placed near
" Newarp-sand. With respect to my own
" opinion, I am happy to find it agrees with
" your own, and those gentlemen who you
" say, propose to apply to the Trinity House
" here, for the purpose of putting the plan into
" execution. If I can render you any service
" in it, you may freely communicate your
" wishes; but I apprehend where one owner of
" a ship is interested (in such an alteration on
" that part of the coast) here, you have fifty
" within the port of Newcastle, and all you
" want is a proper number to give your peti-
" tions to the Trinity House *a sufficient weight.*
" You will no doubt, consider, that whatever
" you apply for *to them, must be paid for, by*
" *the shipping using the North Sea trade, by*
" *a tax on the tonnage, per voyage,* and when

"you have obtained the consent of a great
"number of ship-owners, I have no doubt but
"the elder brothers will attend to your peti-
"tion. The same petition you forward from
"Shields, if sent to me, I will get as many sub-
"scribers to it as I can. Indeed there does not
"seem any probability of an opposition to a
"plan of this kind, unless it is to the expence
"of it, which perhaps may be got over, by con-
"vincing those interested of its utility. With
"respect to the removal of Caistor lights, *or
"any other already established*, you probably
"may meet with an opposition to such a plan,
"notwithstanding you may have very good
"reasons to give on the little service they
"are of.

"If I can be of further service to you in this
"business, I will attend to your further letters,
"and remain.
    "Dear Sir, your obliged,
     "And humble Servant,
      "THOMAS HALL,"

"Mr Henry Taylor,
 "Dockwray Square,
  "North Shields.

" N. B. Pray excuse haste, as I could not
" spare time to write you more fully.

" If a committee are appointed, and they
" wish to know what expence per ton will be
" laid on the shipping, for the erection of the
" lights, &c. I will send them down an estimate,
" which will serve for their government, before
" they make their application to the ship-
" owners."

(No. 2.)

TRINITY HOUSE, SCARBOROUGH.

November, 26, 1789.

" Sir,
" Your favour of the 19th instant, together
" with the plan for the erection of additional
" lights for Hasboro' Gatt, and placing a
" beacon upon the south-end of Baldsey Sand,
" have been taken into consideration by a meet-
" ing of the owners of ships at this port; and I
" have it in charge to acquaint you, that they
" are unanimously of opinion, that *these* will be
" of infinite service to the navigation, and that
" they will be very ready to unite in an appli-
" cation to the Trinity House at London, to
" promote the same with all possible expedi-

" tion; but they are at the same time of opin-
" ion, that a floating light *also* placed at the N.
" E. part of the Cockle, would be an additional
" security to the trade; and in this case, the
" Caistor lights might be taken away as un-
" necessary.

I am, Sir,
" Your most obedient Servant,
" WILLIAM WILLIAMSON,
" Clerk of the Trinity House."

" Mr Henry Taylor,
" North Shields.

(No. 3.)

TRINITY HOUSE, HULL.

December 26, 1789.

" Sir,
" Your letter of the 27th ult, and also a
" letter from Mr William Foster, of Bridling-
" ton, enclosing the plan for placing a floating
" light, &c. near Hasboro' Church, were duly
" received by this House: and though you
" have not been answered earlier, the Board
" took the matter into immediate consideration;
" but, desirous of being informed whether the
" Trinity House of Newcastle had been con-
" sulted on the business, wrote to that body;

" and so soon as information was obtained as
" to that, the corporation entirely approving of
" the plan, directed a letter to be wrote to that
" effect to the Trinity House at Deptford
" Strond, recommending the intended improve-
" ments to navigation to be taken into conside-
" ration, and if approved, to be carried into im-
" mediate effect.

" I am, Sir,
" Your obedient Servant,
(Copy) " J. GREEN, Sec."
" Mr Henry Taylor.

(No. 4.)

Whitby, 1st, December, 1789.

" Esteemed Friend,

" Agreeable to thine of the 27th ult. I have
" called a general meeting of the owners and
" masters of ships, belonging to this port, and
" laid before them the plan and proposals from
" the ship-owners of North Shields, for erect-
" ing lights near Mockbegger, placing a float-
" ing light near the north-end of the Newarp,
" placing a buoy on the south-end of Baldsey
" Cliff; and have the pleasure to say, these
" proposals have met their unanimous appro-
" bation. A committee is appointed to join

" the gentlemen of Shields, &c. in an applica-
" tion to the Trinity House, that these useful
" and necessary regulations may be carried into
" execution as early as possible. I am in haste
" to save post.

" Address all letters relative to this busi-
" ness, to John Marshall, Attorney.

" Thy respectful Friend,
" JOHN CHAPMAN."

" Henry Taylor,
 " North Shields.

(No. 5.)

CERTIFICATES OF THE SHIP-OWNERS OF
NORTH SHIELDS,

September 3, 1792.

" Having lately heard that an elder bro-
" ther of the Trinity House, Deptford Strond,
" a few days after the violent storm in Octo-
" ber, 1789, wrote to a ship-owner of this
" place, recommending a plan for lighting
" Hasboro' Gatt, similar to that recommended
" to us by Henry Taylor, of this town; we
" who are ship-owners resident in North
" Shields, and the parish of Tynemouth,
" hereby certify, that we never, till long after

"the said plan was executed, heard of any
"correspondence on the subject of lighting
"Hasboro' Gatt between any member of the
"Trinity House, and a ship-owner of this
"town or neighbourhood; and are of opinion,
"that no such letter was received. Of this
"however we are sure, that no such letter was
"communicated to any of us; and we are
"further of opinion, that no such letter was
"received by any person here; for, if it had,
"it is hardly possible, considering the impor-
"tance of the subject, and the recent loss for
"want of such lights, that it should not have
"been made public.

"John Reed   John Cunningham
"Alex. Crighton Thomas Kettlewell
"Wm. Richardson John Railston
"Cockerill Deighton John Tavenor
"William Coppin Alex. Bartleman
"Wm. Mitcalfe, Jun. Thomas Chaters
"James Smith   John Fenwick
"Stephen Wright E. C. Millburn
"Samuel Hurry Quintin Blackburn
"John Walker   William Clark
"Robert Laing   Thomas Cannaway

" William Apedaile   William Curry
" S. Wright, Jun.   Thomas Wright
" John Scott   William Harrison
" George Brown   John Noble
" George French   William Taylor
" Thomas Fenwick   John Robinson
" Joseph Sabourn   William Royall
" Thomas Tinley   Robert Brown"

TRINITY HOUSE, LONDON,

11th March, 1790.

" Sir,

" In order that the matter of the several applications to this corporation, requesting a floating light to be placed at the north-end of the Newarp, and for other lights, &c. may be proceeded on, it is the unanimous opinion of several members of this House, that it would much facilitate the business, and save time, if a deputation of one or more gentlemen (as thought proper) were to be appointed from each port, to have a personal consultation at this House upon the subject. To this effect, a letter is written to each of the ports of Whitby, Scarborough, and Hull, and the brethren of this corporation will be ready to receive the

" gentlemen, whenever it is convenient to them,
" upon being favoured with a line, signifying
" what day it will suit them to attend, in order
" that the brethren may be convened.

" I am, Sir,
" Your most humble Servant,
(Copy) " CHARLES WILDBORE*."
" Jonathan Airey, Esq.

Newcastle, 14th March, 1790.
" Sir,
" I enclose your copy of a letter received this
" day from the Trinity House, London, which
" you will communicate to the trade; the con-
" sequence will be an early meeting here of
" the whole trade, of which they will be
" advertised."†

" If, Henry, with your correspondents at
" Hull, Scarborough, and Whitby, you would

---

* The above letter is the first that was received by the Trinity Board, or any of its members, on the subject of lighting Hasboro' Gatt. On the 19th of December, 1789, and not before the business was publicly known in the port of Newcastle, on which day a meeting was held at the Trinity House, when the plan and correspondence were unanimously approved, and the sentiments of the meeting communicated by Captain Airey, to the Trinity Board, London.

† A meeting was held a few days after the receipt of the above letter, at which delegates were appointed, conformable to the request of the Trinity Board, London.

" fix a time for the whole deputations to meet
" in case the proposal is approved, it might
" have its use.
"I am, Sir,
" Your most humble Servant,
" J. AIREY."

" Henry Taylor,
" North Shields.

(No. 6.)

" A statement of the circumstances of fixing
" the floating lights in Hasboro' Gatt, and
" at the north-end of the Goodwin Sands;
" Intended as a testimony of our obligations to
" the Author of the two plans, and of our
" warm approbation of the great pains he
" took to have them carried into execution;
" and for which we consider the shipping
" interest of these kingdoms highly in-
" debted.

" The want of a safe night passage into Yar-
" mouth Roads, or through Hasboro' Gatt, has
" been severely felt by the shipping interest of
" this kingdom.

" Ships that could not save day-light into
" the Roads, or through the Gatt, were obliged

" to anchor under Winterton, or lay-to under
" sail till day.

" To risk a winter-night in such a situation,
" was the dread of the boldest seaman, and for
" a large fleet to lay-to from two o'clock in the
" afternoon, until eight the next morning (as
" has frequently been the case), was not less
" dangerous. Many of the heavy losses that
" have happened hereby, must be in the recol-
" lection of every seamen, particularly that
" dreadful loss in October, 1789, when forty-
" two ships were drove on shore, and on the
" adjacent sands; twenty-three of which were
" totally lost, and most of their crews. This
" event (as might naturally be supposed) threw
" the ship-owners in the North (who were the
" greatest sufferers in this storm) into the
" greatest consternation; and almost every
" one's mind was turned to a consideration of
" some means to prevent the like calamity in
" future: but they were much divided in their
" opinions. The greatest part thought a float-
" ing light should be placed at the north-end
" of the Newarp; others thought it should be
" at the south-end of Hasboro' Sand; some re-
" vived the idea (suggested about twenty years

" ago) of a floating light in the Cockle Gatt;
" and several thought that a light either at the
" Newarp, or south-end of Hasboro' Sand,
" would serve only to lead ships into danger,
" as it was reported and believed by many in-
" telligent people, that a dangerous sand was
" lately grown up in the middle of the Gatt-
" way. Owing to such difference of senti-
" ments, the scheme was likely to die away, as
" the former had done; when Henry Taylor
" of North Shields, produced a rough sketch of
" a plan, which placed a float with three lights,
" one mile N. N. E. from the north-end of the
" Newarp, and two leading lights near Has-
" boro' church, without which it would have
" been unsafe to have entered the Gatt in dark
" nights, when the float could not be seen: be-
" sides those leading lights, direct safely through
" the Gatt-way, if by means of a storm, or o-
" ther accident, the float should be drove a-
" drift.

" The Gatt is now found to be (as he has de-
" scribed it) a wide clear, and safe night pas-
" sage, and spoke of as such, by every intel-
" ligent seaman. Soon after, he conceived the
" idea of another plan, as necessary for the

" preservation of ships and lives as that we
" have now described, but was prevailed on
" by some, not to bring it forward at that time.
" But seeing in the public papers, accounts of
" many ships lost on the Goodwin Sands, he
" published last winter his plan for a float-
" ing light at the north-end of the Goodwin,
" and for removing the North Foreland light, to
" Long-nose Point; this was, if possible, more
" generally approved, than the plan for lighting
" Hasboro' Gatt, and petitions to the Trinity
" House, London, for the execution of it, were
" signed by the master and brothers of the
" Trinity House, and almost every ship-owner
" of this port, the ship-owners of Sunderland,
" Scarborough, Bridlington, and Liverpool,
" the masters and brothers of the Trinity
" House, Hull, also by the ship-owners and
" merchants of that place. We do not exag-
" gerate, when we declare it is our opinion,
" that in consequence of said two plans, many
" ships, and a great number of valuable lives
" will be annaully saved to this country, besides
" the benefits that will accrue to foreigners.

"Newastle, 7th of April, 1792.

"J. Airey, Master of the Trinity House in 1790.
"John Atkinson, Master in 1791.
"John Anderson, Master in 1792.
"Samuel Lawton, chairman of the committee
"of the ship-owner's association.
"Present and former committee of ship-owners
"of the port of Newcastle.

"John Walker	Henry Shadforth
"James Smith	Alex. Rutherford
"Thomas Ware	T. E. Headlam
"John Scott	William Row
"John Fenwick	Robert Yelloley
"John Salmon	Quintin Blackburn
"Michael Rockwood	S. Wright, Jun.
"William Clark	Samuel Hurry."

(No. 7.)

TO THE FRIENDS OF HUMANITY, AND THOSE IN-
TERESTED IN SHIPPING AND COMMERCE.

About three years ago, application was made to the Trinity House, London, for a floating light at the north-end of the Goodwin Sands; this application was, perhaps, more general than any one made at any former period, on any account whatever, to that house.

The ship-owners of the port of Newcastle, including the master and elder brethren of the Trinity House there, the ship-owners of Sunderland and Scarborough, the Trinity Board, merchants, underwriters, and ship-owners of Hull, as well as several other places, sent memorials to the Trinity House, London, stating the benefits that would accrue to navigation and commerce, from such a floating light, and earnestly pressing the execution of the plan (which accompanied the memorials); but all these memorials were unattended to, until about the middle of the year 1792, when a meeting was held at the London Tavern on the occasion.

The Trinity Board then agreed to comply with the wishes of the shipping interest, but as the memorials which the trade had sent, were not in the usual form, the said Board ordered copies taken from a form of their own, to be sent to the several maritime ports (which were readily signed by the ship-owners, and returned to the said Board), from which the following is extracted.

" Whereas the Sands commonly called the
" Goodwin Sands, on the coast of the county

"of Kent, form many dangerous shoals, and many ships and cargoes have been lost thereon, and great numbers of brave seamen, have there untimely perished, and the lives, ships, and goods of his Majesty's subjects continue exposed to like calamity; and whereas such dangers *might be prevented*, or in a great degree lessened, by a light or lights kept constantly burning, and exhibited during the night-time, at or near the Goodwin Sands, &c."

The author of this essay, anxious for the preservation of the lives of seamen, and the safety of navigation, resquests that the Trinity Board will condescend to give the trade at large their reasons for deferring the execution of a plan confessed by themselves to be necessary to the preservation of the *lives, ships, and goods of his Majesty's subjects.* Indeed every person who reads Lloyd's List, must be convinced of the necessity of such a light as has been strongly recommended, and so earnestly solicited; for there is annually lost on the said sands, property to a great amount, as well as *the lives of his Majesty's subjects.*

The following is taken from the said Lists, from the 12th to the 26th of last November inclusive:

" November 12th, the Minerva, Charleton, a transport, struck on the Goodwin Sands.

The Madona, Allarice, is wrecked on the Goodwin Sands, the captain and fourteen men drowned.

15th. The Ariel, Halberg, is lost on the Goodwin Sands.

19th. The Ninnson, Krag, is carried into Ramsgate, after being upon the Goodwin Sands.

26th. The Fair Lady, from Hambro' to Lisbon, is got upon the Goodwin Sands and it is thought will be lost."

Now had the light been placed comformable to the earnest desire of the trade, it is more than probable that the above, and many more losses had been prevented. There is therefore reason to query, why was it not done: since the necessity and utility of the measure is acknowledged on all hands, even by the Trinity Board themselves? Perhaps they are waiting till the poor individual who projected the plan is forgotten.

Many were in hopes that the surveying of the said sands, lately made by the Trinity Board, and published in newspapers, fore part of last month, was preparative to their placing the light; but the account is given in so unusual a stile, and so unseamanlike a manner, that one would incline to think it a burlesque on the Trinity Board, rather than as seriously done by them for the information of mariners. The following is copied from the Hull Packet, August the 12th.

" The London papers of last week give the
" following paragraph:

" The Trinity Board, in their nautical re-
" searches of the present summer, have disco-
" vered by the most accurate soundings of
" (what are denominated) the Goodwin Sands,
" adjoining to the Downs, a spacious deep bay
" nearly in the *centre* of them, capable of affor-
" ding safe riding for the largest ships in all
" weathers.—This bay they have ordered to be
" marked out immediately, with the necessary
" buoys and beacons.

" By this valuable discovery, our mariners
" will now find a safe anchorage in that lati-

"tude of our coast, where hitherto they have
"only looked for a watery grave!!!"

Of what use are bays and swatches in those sands? It were better there were none, but that the North and South Sands were united, and raised so high as not to be overflowed by the highest spring-tides. The Downs would then be a safer road-stead than it now is, and if in those bays or swatches ever so many buoys or beacons were placed, they would not prevent one shipwreck during night, *because they could not be seen*. A floating light therefore is the only means of preventing such frequent losses of men and property, as have heretofore happened on those fatal sands.

It has been said, as an excuse for the light not being placed during the present war, that it would be of advantage to privateers, who might be so audacious as to attempt to cut vessels out of the Downs, for it would direct them through the Gull-stream. And would it not give our cruisers the same advantage in pursuit of them? Every body that has used the sea, knows there is not the least difficulty in entering the Downs from the Southward in the darkest night, and very little in running out through the Gull-stream in moderate weather and a clear night; and I am fully persuaded, the captain of a privateer, who knows the situation of the sands adjacent to the Downs (and one may be assured no other would attempt it), would rather attempt to cut a vessel out of the Downs now, than when the light is placed; he might easily grapple his way through the Gull-stream, when none of our crusiers durst follow for want of light.

There does not appear one solid reason why the floating light should not be immediately placed; but many weighty ones for its being done immediately: the expence is no object, and if it was, they who solicit it will have to pay it.

The bare interest of the property lost on the Goodwin Sands *in one year*, would maintain a floating light for a century.

To give more weight to this address, I take the liberty to say, that by intelligent mariners, the floating light at the Goodwin is thought of equal importance to the lighting of Hasboro' Gatt, and of what importance the lighting that Gatt is, may be gathered from the concurrent testimonies of all who pass that way, and particularly by the following striking circumstance.

In the night of the 31st of October, 1789, twenty-three ships, and about three hundred seamen, were lost; at the same time, twenty more ships were driven on the strand and sands adjacent, and were got off with considerable damage. This calamity was chiefly owing to the want of a safe night-passage through Hasboro' Gatt, or into Yarmouth Roads, which always obliged ships to anchor under Winterton till day-light. But since the Gatt has been lighted, which it has been near four years, I do not know that one ship has been lost for want of a sure guide through the Gatt-way.

I have in my possession a letter from the Secretary of the Trinity House, advising that about three months after the Gatt was lighted, *one hundred sail of ships went through it safely in one night.* The wind was then Northerly, the most dangerous of all winds on that coast, and had not the Gatt been open as a night-passage, they must all have anchored under Winterton, or lay-to under sail, waiting for day, and many of them would probably have been lost before morning.

It is to be feared, that many will use all their influence with the warden of the Cinque ports (who is also master of the Trinity House), to prevent a measure so destructive of their gain; they will probably represent to him, that no vessel can ride out the storms in so exposed a situation, and that the light-vessel will frequently break a-drift and drown all the people; and, *as he is no seaman himself*, he will doubtless believe them. When the ship-owners in the North sent me to London in 1792, to solicit the Trinity Board for the light, that Board, in their examination of me, said the same, that the light-vessel would not ride, but would drown all the people. I told them I was a seaman, I knew better, and should have no objection to stay on board of her the first six months.

The season is now approaching, when long nights and stormy weather will make the navigation of the Kentish-well as dangerous as it has always been during winter.

The Trinity Board is therefore called upon by their duty and their promise, by the interests of shipping, and the calls of humanity, to place a floating light at the north-end of the Goodwin Sands, without further loss of time.

HENRY TAYLOR.

North Shields,
9th Month, Sept. 29, 1794.

(No. 8.)

TO THE MASTER AND ELDER BRETHREN OF THE TRINITY HOUSE DEPTFORD STROND.

THE RESPECTFUL PETITION OF H. TAYLOR,
Sheweth,

That your petitioner has used the sea twenty-one years, great part of which time he commanded ships, chiefly in the coal-trade, but is now resident on shore at North Shields; and having turned much of his attention to the improvement of navigation, the security of commerce, and especially to the preservation of the lives of seamen, near the end of the year 1789, he proposed a plan for opening a night passage through Hasboro' Gatt, which being approved by all the shipping interest of the North, they petitioned your House for the execution of it, and meeting with your approbation also, was carried into effect in the year 1790. It is unnecessary for your petitioner to expatiate on the benefits that will accrue to commerce, to ships, and to seamen; suffice it to say, that it is the unanimous opinion of professional men, that the lighting of Hasboro' Gatt has been, and will continue to be, the means (under Providence) of annually saving many ships and lives.

Your petitioner being encouraged by this favorable reception of his plan for lighting Hasboro' Gatt, has since suggested, that the same principle may, with the same good effects, be applied to other parts of the coast, and particularly, that most important beneficial consequences would result to the trade of this kingdom, from a similar floating light, placed at the north end of the Goodwin Sands. Accordingly about the middle of last year, he laid his plan before the shipping interests at different maritime ports, who immediately approved the same. They having petitioned your House, that the same may immediately be carried into execution, and a general meeting having been held on this business, at the London Tavern, the 6th ult. all present approved the plan, and signed a petition to your House, and which has since been signed by many respectable merchants and ship-owners, your petitioner cannot but hope, that your House will favor this plan also with its protection.

The shipping interest convinced of the advantages that will result from the execution of the said two plans, have advised your petitioner to apply to your House, who are competent to judge of the merits and utility of the same, and to request that, as a compensation for his successful attention to matters of such public utility, you will please grant him a lease of the proposed Goodwin lights, on such terms as may be deemed proper.

HENRY TAYLOR,

7th Month, 1792.

(No. 9.)

TO THE SHIP-OWNERS, MERCHANTS, AND UNDERWRITERS, OF THE PORT OF LONDON.

Gentlemen,

The many heavy losses which annually happen on the Goodwin Sands, and the sands adjacent, have been severely felt by those interested in the shipping and commerce of this kingdom.

A plan which we conceive well calculated to prevent such loss in future, was about six months ago, laid before us by a resident here, Mr. Henry Taylor, approved by the Trinity House and trade of this port, and a petition presented to the Trinity House, Deptford Strond (signed by almost every principal ship-owner, including the master and brothers of the Trinity House) *for a floating light at the north-end of the Goodwin.* Similar petitions or memorials were sent to the Trinity House from the ports of Sunderland, Scarborough, Bridlington, the Trinity House, merchants, underwriters, and ship-owners of the port of Hull, and by the Chamber of Commerce, Liverpool, praying that the said plan may be carried into execution as soon as possible. The answer from the Trinity Board was to the following purport: " A light at the north-end of the " Goodwin Sands, would be of great benefit to " all descriptions of vessels bound westward, " but that they would not take any steps in " the business until the trade of the port of " London applied for it."

We cannot doubt but (if you take the said plan into consideration) you will see, that when executed, it will be of essential benefit to all that pass by the Goodwin, as well those to and from London, as those that come from, or sail to the north.

We should have thought it an insult to your understandings, to have pointed out situations in which your ships to and from the westward will be benefited by a floating light at the Goodwin, if it had not been suggested to us, that you will oppose the placing of such a light, or paying any thing towards its maintenance, on a supposition that your ships will not need it.

Suppose a fleet of your West-India ships, in the early part of a long night, meet with a storm of wind southerly, between Dungeness and Dover, you know they cannot keep to windward until day light; they dare not run into the Downs, because they believe their anchors and cables will not bring them up; they must then unavoidably, as the case now stands, drive into the Kentish Well, where, being unacquainted, many of them are doubtless lost on the Falls, Galloper, &c. and are no more ever heard of, than if they had foundered in the ocean. Now if a floating light be placed at the north-end of the Goodwin, and a light on Long Nose Point, instead of the North Foreland light, they may run to Margate Roads as safely as with day-light.

Again: If a ship part from her anchors in the Downs the floating light will direct her safely through the Gull-stream. Also, ships from London bound westward, when thwart of Margate, at the close of day, with a northerly wind, would, by the aid of such lights, find their way safely to the Channel, either through the Gull-stream, or without the Goodwin.

This, no doubt, will appear self-evident to you, and that you will unite with us and other ports, in an application to the Trinity Board, for the execution of the said plan without further loss of time. We cannot think this of less consequence than the float and leading lights for Hasboro' Gatt, which in the judgment of well-informed men, will be the means of saving thousands of lives, and millions of property.

As commanders of ships, we have often been in such situations that we would have given nearly all we were possessed of for the benefit of such a light. Experience has taught us how difficult it is to account for a ship's way in narrow channels and cross tides; nor need we tell you, that *there is no part of the coasts of this kingdom so dangerous, or were so many ships are lost, as in the Kentish Well, and the Sands adjacent to it.* We know one person,* who, while he lay in the Downs, saw thirty ships lost on the Goodwin, and does not doubt, but as many were lost in the same space of time on the Flemish Banks and coast of France, either through dread of falling on the Goodwin, or through mistaking one Foreland light for the other; a case that often happens, and is often attended with fatal consequences, but which the floating light will effectually prevent.

The loss of many ships is occasioned by thick or foggy weather, when no lights can be seen; but such loss will, in a great measure, be prevented by the large bell which is proposed to be fixed in the float, and rung day and night in such weather. We think there is only one description of men likely to suffer by the execution of the plan, and that is boatmen from Deal, Ramsgate, and Broad Staits, who live by the misfortunes of others. These men, we are credibly informed, go out with their boats in foggy weather, and range themselves without

---

* John Scott, Esq. one of the subscribers to this paper.

the Goodwin, in full expectation that some unfortunate ship will stumble on the Sand, which they seize as their prey. We shall mention one instance, being in possession of the master's protest. A collier crossing the Kent, with an Easterly wind and thick weather, grounded on the North end of the Goodwin; in about *a quarter of an hour* he was boarded by a Ramsgate boat, in less than *one hour* the ship came off without damage; they took the master on shore and the commissioners awarded the boatmen *sixty guineas*, which, with other charges, amounted to upwards of seventy pounds. We are confident any boatmen belonging to this neighbourhood, would have thought themselves generously paid with three guineas, for three times the trouble the Ramsgate men had.

If such numbers of Deal, Ramsgate, and Broad Stairs boatmen, have little other dependence for a livelihood, than the wreck and salvage that happen near their coasts, it at least implies, that those misfortunes frequently occur, and that every possible means should be made use of to prevent the like in future.

The East India Company, and the owners of

ships employed by them, are very much interested in this business; most of their large ships going round the Long Sand Head, will find great benefit from a floating light at the north-end of the Goodwin.

To ships of war, this light will be of essential service; and we therefore hope that the subject will not be deemed unworthy of the notice of the Lords of the Admiralty: it is unecessary to inform them, that, owing to causes mentioned in the former part of this address, many brave seamen have lost their lives on the Goodwin Sands, and sands adjacent, which, had a floating light been placed as above, might have been saved to their country, their families, and their friends. Independent of particular interests, we conceive that the *interests of humanity and good policy* call loudly for the execution of any plan calculated to save the lives of men.

COMMITTEE OF SHIP-OWNERS OF THE PORT OF NEWCASTLE, 29TH OF JANUARY, 1782.

Michael Rockwood	Thomas Ware
John Cock	John Scott
John Salmon	Stephen Wright, Jun.

John Crofton	Thomas Wright
Joseph Bulmer	Henry Shadforth
Nicholas Fairles	T. E. Headlam
John Wardle	William Row
William Clark	Alex. Rutherford
Samuel Hurry	

SAMUEL LAWTON, CHAIRMAN.

It is matter of astonishment, that the ship-owners, merchants, and underwriters, of the port of London, should have been so inattentive to their interests, as to refuse for such a length of time to unite with the other ports in an application to the Board; and it is no less astonishing, that the Board, with the knowledge expressed in their form of memorial (see No 10), should have refused to comply with the wishes of the other ports on that account.

(No. 10.)

COPY OF THE PETITIONS, WHICH THE TRINITY HOUSE ORDERED TO BE ENGROSSED AND SENT TO THE DIFFERENT PORTS.

Whereas the sands commonly called the Goodwin Sands, on the coast of the county of Kent, form very dangerous shoals, and many ships and vessels with their cargoes have been lost thereon, and great numbers of brave seamen have there untimely perished, and the lives, ships, and goods, of his Majesty's subjects, continue exposed to like calamities. And whereas such dangers might *be prevented, or in a great degree lessened, by a light or lights being constantly kept burning, and exhibited during the night time, at or near the north-end of the said Goodwin Sands.* Now we whose names are hereto subscribed, being merchants, owners, or masters of ships, or others, using or interested in the northern or eastern navigation, do request and desire the master, warden, and assistants of the guild, fraternity, or brotherhood of the most glorious and undivided Trinity, and of St. Clement, in the parish of Deptford Strond, in the county of Kent, to cause a floating light to be placed, maintained, and constantly kept burning and exhibited during the night time, at or near the north-end of the said Goodwin Sand. And do hereby promise, consent, and agree, to pay the said master, warden, and assistants, and their successors for ever, for or towards the charges of placing and maintaining such light or lights as aforesaid, the following tolls and duties: that is to say, for all British ships and vessels (except vessels laden with coals, and coasting vessels), one halfpenny per ton, for every time of crossing or passing by the said light or lights, and for all such ships or vessels laden with coals, one halfpenny per Newcastle chaldron, for every time of crossing or passing by the said light or lights; and double the said tolls or duties for all foreign ships and vessels, for every time of so crossing or passing by the said light or lights, provided that nothing more shall be paid for ships or vessels in the coal trade going coastwise, for the whole voyage, out and home, than the tolls and duties abovementioned; and for every coasting vessel not laden with coals, one shilling for every time of so crossing or passing by the said light or lights.

(No. 11.)

CHAMBER OF COMMERCE, LIVERPOOL,

"*30th July*, 1791.

" Sir,

" Your letter dated the 22d current, contain-
" ing a proposal for erecting a floating light

"at the North end of the Goodwin Sands, "and a light on Long-nose Point, instead of "the North Foreland light, was a few days ago "put into my hands. The masters of vessels "in the cheese trade, from hence to London, "have been consulted, and express the utmost "satisfaction and approbation of the scheme. "I have accordingly prepared a memorial to "the Master, Wardens, and Brethren of the "Trinity House, Deptford Strond, praying "their patronage and assistance therein, so far "as it appears to merit their approbation; sub- "jecting all vessels passing the said lights, to "such moderate duty only, as may be sufficient "to defray the charge of their construction "and support. This memorial goes by to- "night's post to Alderman Curtis, London, as "you have recommended, our own members "being absent from town.

"I have the honour to be, Sir,
"Your obedient humble Servant,

"SAMUEL GREEN, Sec."

"Mr. Henry Taylor,
  "North Shields.

(No. 12.)

TRINITY HOUSE, HULL,

"30th *July*, 1791.

" Sir,

" I am directed to acknowledge the receipt
" of your letter to the wardens, of the 15th
" present, on the subject of a floating light
" near the north-end of the Goodwin, and it
" meeting with the approbation of this Board,
" convened the merchants, underwriters, and
" ship-owners of this town, to take the same
" into consideration and the plan being ap-
" proved of by the meeting, this corporation
" was requested to recommend its being car-
" ried into execution by the Trinity House of
" Deptford Strond.

" I have accordingly by this post, acquain-
" ted that corporation of the scheme having the
" approbation of the maritime trade here, as
" well as of this House, and requested the
" same being adopted, provided it can be effec-
" ted without creating too heavy a burthen on
" trade.

" This corporation think your exertions for
" the improvement of navigation highly com-
" mendable, and doubt not, but the concerned
" in shipping have a due sense of your laudable

" endeavours towards the preservation of lives,
" and security of property.

" I have the honour to be,
" Sir, Your obedient humble Servant,
" J. Green, Sec."
" Mr. Henry Taylor.

(No. 13.)

TRINITY HOUSE, SCARBOROUGH,
8th May, 1792.
" Sir,

" The ship-owners of the port of Scar-
" borough, being perfectly convinced of the
" peculiar benefits which the commerce and
" navigation of this kingdom, and especially
" of the northern ports, have received from the
" plan of lighting Hasboro' Gatt, return their
" sincere thanks to Mr Henry Taylor, of
" North Shields, for his particular zeal and
" exertions, in promoting, and bringing to
" conclusion, a business of such national
" utility.

" They are also unanimously of opinion, that
" the proposed light at the Goodwin, and re-
" moving the light on the North Foreland to
" Long Nose Point, if carried into execution,
" will be attended with the most beneficial

"consequences to the maritime interests of
"this country, and may be the means of pre-
"serving a considerable amount of property,
"and a great many valuable lives, from being
"lost on these sands, and the sands adjacent;
"and they request that Mr. Henry Taylor
"prosecute his endeavours, to obtain the ac-
"complishment of an object of so very great
"importance, which the sooner it is effected the
"better it will be for the essential interest of
"navigation: and they at the same time as-
"sure him that his success will meet their ap-
"probation.

"We are, Sir,
"Your most humble Servants,
"ROBERT WARDROBE, President."
"Mr Henry Taylor,
"North Shields.

(No. 18.)

TRINITY HOUSE, LONDON,
8th February, 1791.

"Sir,
"I have the directions of this corporation to
"acquaint you, that the brig Friend's Adven-
"ture, William Guest, master (of which they

" are informed you are the managing owner),
" ran athwart the hawse of the floating light
" vessel, placed by this corporation in Hasboro'
" Gatt, as a guide to navigation, on Sunday,
" the 23d instant, at ten o'clock at night, and
" broke her away from her moorings; and the
" corporation's agent at Yarmouth, being on
" board the light vessel at the time, it being
" clear and moon-light, called to Mr Guest
" several times, and received answers from him
" before the brig struck the light-vessel, and
" therefore, that the master is left without ex-
" cuse for committing this act, which at once
" deprived one hundred sail of vessels, passing
" through the Gatt, that night, of the benefit of
" this light; and the master, on his arrival in
" the river, instead of coming to this House,
" and acknowledging his concern for his bad
" conduct, used every means to prevent its be-
" ing known; and it was not till a reward of
" twenty guineas was offered, that the corpo-
" ration could get fully possessed of the infor-
" mation necessary to ascertain that the Friend's
" Adventure was the identical vessel that did
" this damage, and which Mr Guest, on his be-

"ing sent for, and attending at this House to-
"day, has acknowledged.

"The corporation farther direct me to
"acquaint you, that the moorings of the light-
"vessel are not yet found, but that great ex-
"penses have already been incurred, and fur-
"ther charges will attend the re-mooring her,
"an account of which will be sent you as soon
"as it can be obtained; that the greatest con-
"cern which the corporation, as well as all the
"ship-owners must, and ought to feel, on this
"occasion, is the risk navigation has been ex-
"posed to, during the time the lights could not
"be exhibited; and they therefore command
"me to inform you, as the managing owner of
"this brig, with the circumstances attending
"the matter, in expectation of your immediate
"answer, which may be the means of prevent-
"ing farther trouble and expenses to yourself,
"and the other owners of the Friend's Ad-
"venture.

"I am, Sir,
Your most humble Servant,
"CHARLES WILDBORE,"

"Mr George Denholm,
"South Shields.

(No. 15.)

Sunderland, May 3, 1792.

" Sir,

" The ship-owners of this port being sensible
" of the great advantage that has arisen to the
" commerce and navigation of this kingdom,
" and especially of the northern ports, from
" your plan for lighting Hasboro' Gatt, wish
" to offer you their thanks for the invention,
" and the great diligence and zeal with which
" you prosecuted that business to a conclu-
" sion.

" The ship-owners are unanimously of opin-
" ion, that your plan for placing a floating
" light at the north-end of the Goodwin
" Sands, and removing the light on the North
" Foreland to Long Nose Point, will, if car-
" ried into execution, be of the greatest nation-
" al utility, by being the means of preserving
" many thousands of property annually lost on
" those sands, and sands adjacent, as well as
" the lives of many of their fellow creatures.
" They therefore request you not to relax in
" your endeavours to obtain the accomplish-
" ment of so desirable an end, which they

" sincerely wish may be speedily effected, and
" that some plan may be adopted to reward
" the great service you have rendered your
" country, in which they will most heartily
" concur.

     " We remain, Sir,
    " Your most obedient Servants,
" William Havelock Thomas Lipton
" Tho. Nicholson Robert Allan
" Robert Hutton Edward Aiskell."
  Committee of Ship-Owners.
" Mr Henry Taylor,
" North Shields.

(No. 16.)

" The trade of the port of Newcastle, being
" under great obligations to Henry Taylor,
" of North Shields, for the plan of the floating
" light at the Goodwin Sands, as well as for
" the lights of Hasboro' Gatt, earnestly recom-
" mended it to the Trinity House, Deptford
" Strond, to grant him a lease of, at least, one
" of the floating lights.
" Samuel Lawton John Fenwick
" William Clark James Walmsley
" T. E. Headlam Patrick Holland
" John Wardle   Quintin Blackburn

" Alex. Rutherford William Reay
" William Row Thomas Fenwick
" Henry Shadforth Robert Brown, Jun.
" Nicholas Fairles Thomas Chaters
" S. Wright, Jun. E. C. Milburn
" George Cram Francis Blackett
" Rowland Hodge Henry Robinson
" John Walker R. Bulmer & Co.
" Henry Anderson Henry Heath
" Stephen Wright Joseph W. Roxby
" John Liddell Nicholas Teasdale
" W. Mitcalfe, Jun. Charles Wilson
" John Reed T. Powditch
" William Harrison Thomas Robertson
" William Reed Robert Dobby
" John Scott S. Temple, Jun.
" Alex. Crighton John Watson
" W. Poppelwell Robert Burton
" Alex. Bartleman William Taylor
" James Smith John Wallis
" Peter Shields John Salmon
" James Lyon Michael Rockwood
" E. A. Major James Downey
" John Stephenson John Railston
" William Wallis John Chapman

(No. 7.)

TRINITY HOUSE, SCARBOROUGH.

"*July* 30, 1792.

"The ship-owners of this port of Scarborough are very much obliged to Mr. Henry Taylor, of North Shields, for the plan of a floating light at the Goodwin, as well as for lighting Hasboro' Gatt, which is of very essential service in general, but more particularly to the Northern navigation: We, the undersigned, judging it an act of justice to real merit, that such laudable exertions should be suitably rewarded, do request, that such compensation be made by the Trinity House, Deptford Strond, as to that corporotion should seem just and reasonable, for the many services he has rendered his country.

"Robert Wardrobe   John Smith
"John Hugall   William Smith
"William Herberts   Robert Jackson
"William Sollitt   Thomas Sheraton
"W. Maxwell   Samuel Bortch
"Robert Cossirs   John Herbert
"R. Williamson   George Todd
"Val. Fowler   John Williamson

" Thomas Colley   Frederick Cornwall
" William Kemeys   John Fox, Jun.
" William Chambers   J. N. Vikerman
" Francis Bentley   John Hopper
" Thomas Haggitt   George Hawson
" Joseph Cockerill   George Hawson, Jun.
" Nesfield Fletcher   John Dutchman
" John Parkin   George Fowler
" W. Williamson   Thomas Thornton
" W. Wharton   George Fowler, Jun.
" James Tindall   Hugh Pickering
" John Cockerill   Benjamin Heward

Scarborough, Jan. 7, 1793.

" Sir,

" This day I received yours, and observed
" its contents. I certainly should have sent
" this, if I had not received a letter from you,
" informing me, that I should have a form of
" a petition from London, and that some per-
" son was to see the signatures put to it, and
" attested by him; but they neglected to send to
" us, as to other ports, was the reason of us
" sending so late, which reason I sent to the
" Trinity House, London, along with the
" petition.

"I shall consult, the ship-owners of this port, respecting the association, and shall advise you.

"I am, Sir,
"Your most humble Servant,
"ROBERT WARDROBE."

"Mr Henry Taylor,
"North Shields.

(No. 18.)

In July, 1792, the following paper was sent from the brethren of the Trinity House, the merchants, and ship-owners of Hull, to the Trinity House, Deptford Strond.

"Mr Henry Taylor, of North Shields, being the projector of the annexed plan, as also that of lighting Hasboro' Gatt, which is of very essential service to the northern navigation:

"We, the undersigned, conceiving it no more than an act of justice to real merit, that such laudable exertions should be suitably rewarded, do request that such compensation be made him by the Trinity House, Deptford Strond, as to that corporation shall seem just and reasonable,

" William Burstal   C. E. Broadley
" Thomas Brown   Skipsey, Son, & Co.
" Thomas Hawerth   T. A. Terrcughn
" John Staneforth   John Boyes
" W. Therley   Thomas Scatcherd
" R. McFarland   Thomas Hewson
" Thomas Jackson   John Levett
" Robert Shonswar   Crose, Escrect, & Co.
" B. Metcalf   Thomas Taylor
" C. Shipman   Hugh Ker
" Thomas Lundie   Jonas Brown
" James Frank   John Robertson
" Maisters & Co.   John Newbald
" Lee & Willon   Ralph Turner
" Banks & Foster   John Dobson
" Richard Terry   Samuel Hall
" Atkinson & Co.   John Masterman
" Richard Atkinson   Robert Cowham
" Wilberforce & Co.   Robert Kellock
" William Wray   Wray & Co.

N. B. Besides the above forty, there were other forty-seven signatures, in all, eighty-seven.

P

(No. 19.)

Blyth, 20th Sept. 1792.

" Sir,

" Although the owners and masters of ships
" belonging to the port of Blyth, have been
" later than others in expressing their appro-
" bation of your plans of lighting Hasboro'
" Gatt, they are not less sensible of your merits,
" nor of the advantage that will accrue to na-
" vigation in general, and to us in particular.

" They therefore take this opportunity of
" thanking you, for the essential services that
" this nation have, and will receive from your
" inventions, and they heartily wish that you
" may receive a compensation adequate to
" to your merits.

" We are, Sir

" Your humble Servants,

" William Harrison	William Jordan
" John Marshall	Jeremiah Clarke
" Mark Marshall	Edmund Hannay
" John Milburn	John Story
" Edward Watts	John Clark
" Robert Stoker	Thomas Harrison
" T. Eglington	Joseph Ramsay
" Thomas Gibson	William Briggs

" James Bailey	Matthew Wilson
" William Bates	William Greeves
" Thomas Nurse	Thomas Burry
" William Colery	Charles Byers
" Henry Taylor	Thomas Wilson
" John Steel	Robert Greenwell
" G. Richardson	Peter Brad
" Thomas Ayre	Edward Wright

" Mr Henry Taylor,
" North Shields.

H. T. wrote Captain Thomas Hall, to know if he ever heard any of the Elder Brethren pretend to the merit of giving a plan for lighting Hasboro' Gatt, and received the following reply.

(No 20.)

NO. 17, LONDON ROAD, LONDON,
September 20, 1792.

" Dear Sir,
" I received your letter of the 11th instant
" in course, and I have since made a search for
" your letters, dated 1789, and 1790, on the
" subject you mention; and also for copies of
" mine to you, the former of which I have by
" me, the latter I cannot meet with, therefore I

" conclude that I did not keep any such copies.
" As it is so long ago since this matter com-
" menced, I can only recollect that I took your
" plan and letter to the late Secretary at the
" Trinity House, and communicated your sen-
" timents, and also my own, to him, on the sub-
" ject of the lights; and that several of the
" Elder Brothers, in passing through the Sec-
" retary's room, took notice of the observations,
" but not particularly interested themselves
" therein. The Secretary told me, the Board
" would consider of it, when he laid the plan
" before them; and some time afterwards he
" called upon me, to inform me, that the Tri-
" nity House here, and at Newcastle, had en-
" tered into a correspondence on that business,
" and which he said would be carried into ex-
" ecution. My own affairs taking up the whole
" of my time, I never had an opportunity of
" calling afterwards, to know how matters
" went on, neither did the Secretary call upon
" me again.

" In answer to that part of your letter, ask-
" ing me, whether I ever heard any of the
" Elder Brothers say, that the plan was their
" own, *I never did*; and I will also inform you,

"*that you were the first person that mentioned
 the subject to me.* I was interested in the
 measure, in consequence of the importance
 of it, and, had it been necessary, I should
 have used all my interest to forward the
 design.

" I remain, &c.
" THOMAS HALL."

" Mr Henry Taylor,
 " North Shields.

(No. 21.)

ADDRESS TO SHIP-OWNERS.

The respectful attention which you have piad to my former addresses on similar subjects, encourages me to hope for your candid attention to this.

Lights are for direction in the night; and of all lights, those that float are confessedly the best, because if doubtful of your distance, you can approach within hail; but how often have we been deceived in our distance from lights on land, by the state of the atmosphere, and the brightness or dimness of the fires.

One floating light seems wanting (exclusive of the Goodwin light, which though not yet placed, is promised to be soon) to make the navigation of the coast between this, the river Thames, and South Foreland, as secure as it well can be made; and that light should be near the end of the Sunk Sand, suppose two miles N. E.

To make use of many arguments to convince such ship-owners as are real professional men, would be to insult their understandings.

That the King's Channel has not been more frequented by loaded, as well as light ships, has often been a matter of astonishment to me, and no doubt to many others. We have often known fleets of light colliers, that have saved day-light round the middle, with the wind Southerly, instead of continuing a straight course down Swin, and without the Shipwash, have grappled their way in at the Slead, and been obliged to bring up in the bay, the wind not being free enough to sail out at the Ness. Strange infatuation! Owing no doubt to that *tyrant custom*, or to the too little use of the compass and the log in the coasting trade; if, however, a floating light was placed as above I should hope to hear that the Sleadway is as little frequented as the Cockle Gatt has been, since the lighting of the Hasboro' Gatt.

A floating light at the East end of the sunk, would be not only a safe guide through the King's Channel, but also of singular service to ships crossing the Kent, as by the bearing of it, they would know when they had passed the Long Sandhead, and the Kentish-knock. To loaded ships sailing through the Slead, with the wind Westerly, it would shew them how far they may stand off; great numbers of ships by tacking too soon, especially with the wind far Southerly, have been unexpectedly hurried, by lee wind and lee tide, upon the Gunfleet Sand.

A light at the east-end of the Sunk, is much more necessary now than thirty or forty years ago, because, in those days, commanders of ships were more prudent and cautious than they are now; a man would then have been as much blamed for running further out, than to bring Harwich lights open off the Cliff, as he now is for not running out, be the night ever so dark.

Is this difference respecting sailing in the night, owing to superior knowledge in the present generation? By no means. Ships were formerly better conducted, commanders more respected, seamen better disciplined, and all much more comfortable in their respective situations than at this day; the principal reason why such desperate risks are run, is, that ships are generally insured too near their value.

I am aware that an objection will be made to the measure of another floating light, on the score of expence; but as my plan proposes its being done without any additional imposition, that objection falls to the ground.

I need not tell you that Winterton light is not only unnecessary, but a real nuisance, since the two lights were erected near Hasboro' Church; you pay a penny per chaldron for Winterton, one half of which will be sufficient to maintain a floating light. But you will be told that the light at Winterton is private property; if the proprietor's grant gives him the exclusive privilege of those lights *whilst ships stood in need of them*, it surely was never intended that they should be paid for when they are *really injurious!*

Whoever is the proprietor of these lights, he has been sufficiently paid, having received many thousands of pounds more than the erections and maintenance has cost him. If, however, you cannot obtain your object, unless some compensation is made him, let him receive a halfpenny per chaldron, and make' dove-cots of his light-houses, the other halfpenny will be found amply sufficient for the maintenance of a floating light.

We are taught to believe, that the Trinity Board was constituted not only for the purpose of a general superintendency of navigation, but also for removing old and useless lights, and erecting new ones, beacons, buoys, &c. but of late they have declared on several occasions, that they never make such alterations but at the request of the trade; had ship owners known this fifty years ago, how many losses might have been prevented, that have happened through the badness of Cromer and other lights, and the darkness of Hasboro' Gatt.

If we have to pay so excessively high for lights, why should they not be good ones, and those placed in the most eligible situations, and such as are no longer useful, removed out of the way.

Cromer light is lately made a good one, but it resembles an *ignis fatuus*, for its rotations are so quick, that it does not appear long enough in sight to give time to set it with any degree of certainty. At the request of a ship-owner in Shields, I wrote to the Board on the necessity of making the rotations slower; the answer I received was, that they could make no alterations unless the trade applied for it; if then you think this an objection, you will notice it in your application for the removal of Winterton lights, and for a floating light at the east-end of the Sunk; should you think neither the one or the other necessary, I shall nevertheless feel a satisfaction in having called your attention to a measure which I think of great utility.

HENRY TAYLOR.

3d Mo. 22, 1795.

(No 22.)

TO THE HONOURABLE THE MASTER, WARDENS, AND ELDER BRETHREN, OF THE TRINITY HOUSE, DEPTFORD STROND.

We the undersigned ship-owners, merchants, and underwriters of the port of Newcastle upon Tyne, having had under consideration, the means of preventing the loss of ships and the lives of seamen, on the sands in, and adjacent to the Swin; and desirous of having the King's Channel more frequented than it has hitherto been, beg leave to request, that a floating light, with two lanterns, may be placed about two miles N. E. from the east-end of the Sunk Sand.

A light so situated will, we are assured, contribute essentially to the prevention of many losses; it will make the King's Channel as safe during night, and indeed safer than it now is with day-light, and we conceive it necessary that a white buoy should be placed at the Long Sand Head; and a black buoy at the west-end of the Shipwash, to facilitate the passage between that Sand and Baudsey, which would then be frequented with scant winds. We beg leave respectfully to request, that as Winterton lights are rendered entirely useless, since the opening of Hasboro' Gatt, they may be taken away, which will enable you to afford us a floating light at the east-end of the Sunk, without any additional tax on shipping. It will be extremely hard indeed, if we are to continue to be taxed for lights that are injurious instead of being useful, as the lights at Winterton really are; we trust you will at once see the utility of the measure we now solicit; it will be of singular service to ships crossing the Kent, as well as to those going up or down Swin, as they will know by its bearing, when they pass the Long Sand Head, and the Kentish Knock. To ships of war, and Indiamen, it will be of great service; indeed the benefits that will result from it are so obvious, that we have no doubt but you will think as we do, and grant the request we make, as soon as you can make it convenient.

We beg leave further to request, the favor of a buoy at the north-end of Hasboro' Sand, and that the rotations of Cromer light be made slower; they are now so quick, as not to give time to set it with any degree of accuracy.

Port of Newcastle, April 8, 1795.

NEWCASTLE.

C. Adamson, M. T. H.	George Liddell
Thomas Shadforth	Stephen Atkinson
James John Davis	James Atkinson
George Burdon	M. Headley
Thomas Pearson	Samuel Lawton
Robert Cram	Ralph Atkinson
Anthony Hood	William Boston
L. Robson	John Atkinson
John Airey	T. E. Headlam
George Blaylock	Sol. Chapman

J. Ward
Robert Lisle
R. Jones
John Chapman
Robert Chapman
Purvis Sissons
George Shadforth
William Harle
George Dunn
Thomas Smith

Shallot Dale
William Brown
John Cram
Henry Shadforth
T. Chapman
Robert Gothard
Andrew Morton
Maling Sorsbie
Edward Twizel
William Jackson

SOUTH SHIELDS.

Michael Rockwood
John Wardle
Joseph W. Roxby
Joseph Bulmer
Reeves Wilson
William Reedhead
Joseph Rennoldson
Cuthbert Marshall
Thomas Gibson
John Brown
Thomas Forrest
Thomas Skipsey
John Thompson
Henry Heath

John Henderson
John Watson
R. Bulmer and Co.
Luke Wright
Robert Stephenson
F. Robertson
James Wardle
S. Temple
John Salmon
John Carling
John Roxby
W. T. Miller
Nicholas Fairles
John Marshall

Richard Harrison
Richard Hansell
E. Harper
C. Garbutt
H. Robson
John Headley
Thomas Wallis
John Crofton
Stephen Handcock
Anthony Harrison
William Archer
Thomas Scott
John Stephenson

John Cock
Robert Dobby
Robert Burton
Isaac Scarth
Thomas Scott
George Poad
John Blenkinsop
John Smith
Joseph Hunter
Joseph Robb
Nicholas Teasdale
Francis Jefferson

NORTH SHIELDS.

Stephen Wright
Thomas Wright
W. Mitcalfe, Jun.
John Liddell
George Liddell
Albert Liddell
T. Frank, Jun.
Ralph Richardson
David Smith
Jonathan Smith
Nicholas Bird

Thomas Fenwick
R. Clarke Lowes
W. Clark, Jun.
James Smith
Thomas Chaters
William Harrison
E. C. Milburn
Alex. Crighton
James Lyon
John Reed
William Reed

H. Anderson
Thomas Kettlewell
John Walker
Cockerill Deighton
John K. Graham
Andrew Thompson
William Watt
William Clark
T. Powditch
Thomas Tinley
William Graham
W. Graham, Jun.
George Watson
William Poppelwell
William Reay
M. T. Gilley
John Cunningham
Quintin Blackburn
Alex. Bartleman
George French
W. S. Curry

John Fenwick
Samuel Hurry
George Brown
William Curry
James Sibbald
Francis Fox
William Royal
Robert Dixon
Henry Dixon
David Nixon
Stephen Watson
Henry Taylor
Jacob Robinson
Joseph Sabourn
William Brown
William Richardson
Samuel Price
Thomas Ware
William Young
John Rawson

All the above are ship-owners, and as the light at the Sunk is not yet placed, the names on this memorial are inserted, to shew how unanimous the ship-owners of the port of Newcastle are for its being done; also to prove the uselessness of Winterton lights, and the hardships the trade labours under, by the continuance of the tax for their maintenance. The annexed letter will shew by whom it was handed to the Trinity Board.

(No. 23.)

Portland Place, April 24, 1795.

" Dear Sir,

" I went this morning with Mr Grey and
" Mr. Burdon, to the Trinity House, and pre-
" sented to Mr Preston the memorial of the
" ship-owners, who promised it should be laid
" before the Board, and that I should have
" their determination as soon as possible, which
" you may rest assured, I will transmit to you
" immediately.

" I am, &c.

" CHARLES BRANDLING."

" Mr Henry Taylor,
" North Shields.

(No. 24.)

TRINITY HOUSE, HULL,

July 1, 1791.

" Sir,

" Your letter, accompanied by a requisition
" to the Trinity House Deptford Strond, for

" fixing a floating light near the Long Sand
" Head, was duly received by this House;
" and having, by this House's direction, got the
" requisition generally and respectably signed
" by our merchants and ship-owners, I have
" sent the same to said Trinity House. The
" wardens and gentlemen sincerely wish the
" plan success.

" I am, Sir,
" Your obedient Servant,

" J. GREEN, Sec."
" Mr. Henry Taylor,
" North Shields.

(No. 25.)

TO THE SHIP-OWNERS, MERCHANTS, AND UN-
DERWRITERS, OF THE PORT OF SUNDERLAND.

Trinity House, London, May 7, 1795.

" Gentlemen,
" The corporation of the Trinity House of
" Deptford Strond, having at a general court
" considered your application presented to them
" by Charles Brandling, Charles Grey, and
" Rowland Burdon, Esquires, signifying your
" request, that they will order a floating light

" with two lanterns, to be placed two miles N.
" E. from the east-end of the Sunk Sand, and
" also a white buoy at the Long Sand Head,
" a black buoy at the west-end of the Ship-
" wash, and another buoy at the north-end of
" Hasboro' Sand, for the benefit of navigation.
" And further requesting, that as Winterton
" lights are rendered useless, since the opening
" of Hasboro' Gatt, they may be taken away,
" in order that the floating light may be placed
" at the east-end of the Sunk Sand, without
" any additional tax on shipping: I am com-
" manded to acquaint you, that however desi-
" rous the corporation are, on all occasions,
" to accede to the request of the ship-owners,
" &c. yet one part of this application is conjoin-
" ed with a request, which is not in their
" power to comply with,—the Winterton, as
" well as the Orford lights, being the private
" property of Lord Howard, and which his
" lordship has, within the last four years, either
" rebuilt, or so altered, at a very considerable
" expense, as to improve their utility agreeable
" to the wishes of navigation; for these reasons
" it is persumed, that if the ship-owners are
" desirous that the floating light on the Sunk

" Sand should be immediately established, they will see it necessary for them to make a special application to the corporation for such light, and the three buoys to be placed: signifying therein their readiness to pay to the corporation a toll or duty, adequate to the expense of placing and maintaining the same, in like manner as was agreed to be paid in their request for the floating light in Hasboro' Gatt; and if the ship-owners of the several ports of Newcastle, Sunderland, Stockton, Hull, Whitby, Scarbro', and Yarmouth, will also appoint delegates to confer with the corporation on the business, they will be ready to discuss the points of such application with them, in order that the request of it may be carried into execution without delay.

" With respect to the rotations of Cromer light, which are represented to be so quick as not to give time to set them with any degree of accuracy, I am commanded to acquaint you, that directions will be given for the same to be made slower in future, as soon as it is signified to the corporation in what

" periods of time it is wished the revolutions
" of this light should be made.

" I am, Gentlemen,
"   Your most humble Servant,
"   " DAVID COURT, Sec."

(No. 26.)

Stockton, September 22, 1796.

" Sir,
" We the merchants, ship-owners, and un-
" derwriters of the port of Stockton, being
" truly sensible of the great benefit arising to
" trade and navigation, from your active per-
" severance in promoting floating lights at
" some of the most dangerous and difficult
" places on our coast, can only return you our
" sincere thanks, and hope that so much merit
" will, in some way, receive full compensation
" for the great trouble and expense you have
" had, in lessening the evils of a seafairing life,
" and, we may truly add, in serving so effectu-
" ally the cause of humanity.

" Thomas Simpson   John Barker
   Mayor of Stockton   Joseph Graham
" J. R. Rowntree   Robert Barrett
" Wm. Wetherell   G. Christopher

" Thomas Davison   George Hutchinson
" Benjamin Lumley   Leo. Raisbeck
" Matthew Wadeson   Robert Lumley
" Thomas Wilkinson   R. Christopher
" Thomas Kingston   H. Richardson, sen.
" Jeremiah Eeles   Henry Hutchinson
" Ralph Ware   Richard Walker
" T. Heaviside   James Walker
" Thomas Beckwith   Wm. Wilkinson
" Matthew Crowe   John Rowe
" Charles Engledow   David Clarke

" Mr. Henry Taylor,
  " North Shields.

My worthy friend, R. Burdon, had told the Trinity Board, that if they did not grant me a lease of the lights projected by me, or an equivalent, he would bring the matter before the House of Commons, and he encouraged me to write a narrative, and annex copies of the documents thereto, but finding the opposition too strong to leave a probability of success, he dropped the design, and wrote me, of which the following is a copy:

" In answer to your favour of last week,
" the Deputy Master Rose, told me in our

"interviews this winter, that the Hasboro'
"Gatt light, had been suggested to the Trinity
"House (I think he said) fifty or sixty years
"ago; he spoke of the Goodwin as a matter
"of great difficulty and expense, and seemed
"to doubt the probability of mooring it safely.
"I understood Mr. Pitt had spoken to him.
"I am sorry that the Trinity House should
"*oppose you* in so decided a manner, as to
"render our application, so far as I can
"gather from Messrs Wilberforce, Thornton,
"and others, a measure which will answer no
"good purpose; I shall not, however, dismiss
"it from my mind, and if ever occasion should
"offer to render you service on that ground,
"and in that direction, I shall be glad to em-
"brace it.

"ROWLAND BURDON."

"30 *April*, 1793.

The war continuing, and the Trinity Board still remaining averse to my being rewarded, I wrote my friend Burdon, to drop the thoughts of applying to parliament on my account, and to let the matter rest until more tranquil times, when the passions agitated by war, might be succeeded by calm reflection; and when the less splendid, but more useful arts of navigation and commerce would become the first of national objects.

In the year 1795, I addressed the shipping interests on the necessity of a floating light at the east-end of the Sunk Sand, to faciliate the passage up and down the Swin, and through the King's Channel: this measure was readily given into by the trade; nor did the Trinity House make any objection to it.

Soon after the memorials had gone up, the Board fixed the tax for its maintainance, and sent their own forms to the different ports for signatures, which were easily obtained, and the forms returned to the house.

Esteem and gratitude compels me to bear this testimony to the honour of Rowland Burdon, Esq. that in all my interviews with him on business respecting the lights, I found him to be a sincere and disinterested friend.

1800. We are now come to an end of a most calamitous war, in which the contest was for liberty; but the effect of that contention has produced licentiousness. It was well said by one of the French National Assembly, " A

" nation without morals may acquire liberty,
" but without morals they cannot preserve
" it!"

Liberty is, doubtless, the birth-right of every man, but very few know how to make a proper use of it. Certainly no man can enjoy true liberty but he who has conquered his passions. It allows no man to do that to another that he would not have done to himself. Every man, therefore, who deprives another of his property, or of his life, does not act according to the true nature of liberty. We may exclaim as a great woman did, who suffered the loss of life by the violent asserters of liberty-ill-understood, " O " liberty! how many crimes are committed " in thy name!"

Favoured once more with a general peace, happy will it be for mankind if they see the sin and folly of shedding each other's blood, for no other reason but difference of opinion, and difference of country. Did not God Almighty " *make of one blood all nations of men to dwell* " *on the face of the earth;*" are they not all children (by creation) of one common parent? Then why should they not love one another, however distant or different in colour? and have they not all to give an account of their actions to Him who is of purer eyes than to behold iniquity with approbation, and whose impartiality will respect no man's person?

This year having observed that many ships were lost at the entrance of the harbour of Shields, owing principally to the bad situation of the leading lights, I called the attention of the ship owners to the subject, in consequence of which a general meeting was held on the 2d. of 3d mo. 1805, when the following resolutions were passed unanimously.

" 1st. That the present leading lights, stand
" two far from, and form too great an angle
" with the channel.

" 2d. That application be made to parlia-
" ment for an act, for the purpose of building
" two light houses, removing obstructions to
" a conspicuous view of them, and for defraying
" the expence there be levied one halfpenny
" per ton, per annum on the ships in the port
" of Newcastle.

" 3d. That the thanks of the meeting be
" given to Henry Taylor, for his assiduous at-
" tention to the shipping interests."

The above resolutions being approved by the Trinity house Newcastle, they applied for and obtained the act.

In the early part of 1802, I again wrote my friend Burdon, on the subject of a remuneration from parliament, and to know if he would bring my case before the house of commons, he answered me as follows.

HOUSE OF COMMONS,

Feb. 11, 1802.

" Dear Sir,

" I am duly favoured with yours of the first
" current, and am sorry in answer to assure
" you, that I do not entertain the most distant
" hope of being able to serve you by presenting
" your petition to parliament: As a preli-
" minary, it would be necessary to have his
" Majesty's consent notified to the house by
" the minister, and that would not be obtained
" against the *opinion* of the Trinity House, by
" a person so little versed as I am in nautical
" affairs.

" R. Burdon."

" H. Taylor,
  " North Shields.

William Pitt being removed by death, and a new administration chosen, I was encouraged to make another trial for compensation; accordingly in the early part of 1806, I went to London, Lord Grenville, was first Lord of the Treasury, and also an elder brother of the Trinity House, yet through the kind interference of some of my parliamentry friends, he promised that my petition should be presented to the house, and the speaker had noticed that such petition would be presented, although the time had elapsed for receiving private petitions.

I feel much obliged to William Smith, Esq. M. P. for Norwich, for his assistance in this business; he not only corrected my petition, but gave it to me enclosed in his letter to the Secretary of the Treasury, who on delivering it told me to call in a few days for an answer. Meantime some evil genius had suggested to the Treasury Board, that the petition should be sent to the Trinity House for them to report on it, the petition was accordingly sent, and although the report was void of truth and probability, it induced the minister to *withdraw his promise*, and the secretary was ordered to write me, of which the following is a copy.

" The lights which are stated in your pe-
" tition, to be projected and matured by your
" self, had *many years* before been proposed by
" the Trinity House.

" My lords cannot recommend that his Ma-
" jesty's consent, should be given to the said
" petition being received in the House of com-
" mons.

" N. VANSETTART,
" Treasury Chamber."

" 22 *March*, 1806,

" To Henry Taylor,
" No. 6, Old Jewry.

Now had it been true that the Trinity House proposed those lights, *many years* before, how can they excuse themselves to the trade, for not doing that, which when done, has proved so very advantageous, even in their own opinion?

There is nothing which the Trinity Board have so much cause to dread, as that of being called before the representatives of the people, and, therefore, instead of applying to parliament to impower them to tax the trade for support of the lights in Hasboro' Gatt, they procured through their powerful master, William Pitt, the King's license for that purpose. Is it lawful to tax the people otherwise than through their representatives?

The Trinity Board have now no cause to fear being called to an account, since they have brethren in all the political parties. I am however confident, that if the dukes and lords, who are honorary members of that house, knew how their plebeian brethren have acted, they would think themselves dishonoured by the connection.

The public are ignorant, with regard to the usefulness of the Trinity Board, but intelligent mariners see, that if that house had been always composed of experimental seamen, Hasboro' Gatt had not been without lights sixty years, after the proposal was said to have been made; nor would they have resisted placing a floating light at the north-end of the Goodwin, five years after it was first called for by the general trade; in which time many ships were lost on those dangerous sands. But when at last they thought proper to place the light, they, in order to induce the shipping interest the more cheerfully to pay the tax, which they imposed for its maintenance, magnified the benefits likely to ensue from it, (See the copy of the petition sent by them, for the signatures of the ship owners, No. 10.)

Many years after I settled on shore, I had to struggle with embarrased circumstances, which not without difficulty I weathered through. My heart was always too big for my means; for however I might be oppressed with poverty, I could not resist the propensity, of contributing as much as in my power, towards the happiness of my fellow creatures, especially seamen, for whom I always had a partial regard; and hence, I was ever forward to join in any measures calculated for their benefit.

It will be seen, that I spent many years in schemes of public utility, and no inconsiderable portion of my property; nor did I ever receive the smallest compensation from the ship owners: I dont mean this as a reflection on their justice, or generosity, as they had offered to raise a subscription, which I refused to accept; depending on the Trinity Board for a reasonable remuneration; but no remuneration at all would that Board have given me, not that money was any object with them; but bestowing a reward on me, would have been tacitly to have acknowledged that I merited it.

However, by the interference, and personal intimacy with some of the acting members of the Trinity House, my valuable friends Anthony Brough, and John Walker, Esqrs. procured for me five hundred pounds: to the latter of these gentlemen I have been under such obligations, that without his assistance, I should never have been able to have maintained and educated my numerous family; or have had it in my power to have devoted so large a portion of my time to the service of the public.

The treatise on the management of ships at single anchor having been well received by ship owners, so as to pass through six editions. I was induced in 1787, to print a few general rules for sailing; and, also a short address to seamen.

GENERAL RULES FOR SAILING.

Ships steering or sailing with a fair wind, are always to give way to plying ships; if with daylight, a clear night, and clear weather, the former should run foul of the latter, he is wholly to blame, and the fault is aggravated, if during the night he has either sprit-sail or lower studding sails set, as those are called blind sails, and prevent the master or mate from seeing objects a-head; it will be no excuse to say that seamen were stationed on the forecastle, for the purpose of looking out; because sailors are too generally careless, and often fall asleep. It is always safest to go under the stern of plying ships when near them.

2. Ships sailing different ways with the wind on the beam, are equally in fault if they run foul of each other; but if the one be light and the other loaden, I should lay a greater share of blame on the master of the light ship, because such ships will answer their weather helm very quick, but few loaden ships will do so.

3. If in thick or foggy weather, a steering ship run on board a plying one, provided the former carried a snug sail*, so that she could

---

* On coasts like those of this country, the master of a steering ship should be in constant expectation of meeting with plyers, and therefore in hazy weather should run under such a sail, that his ship could bear close upon a wind.

suddenly be thrown in the wind without danger of losing her masts, and provided each were careful to ring their bells, beat their drums, or sound their horns, I should call the damage done *an act of Providence*, but blame them less or more as they neglected these means, which all careful masters are known to make use of.

4. If two ships plying to windward to the same point or place, where they have sea-room, and fairly under way (provided the weather be clear, or so clear that they may see each other at a cable length distance) run foul of each other, I should consider them equally to blame; but if one of them on such an occasion, when quick exertion is necessary, put his helm a weather, and the other throw his ship immediately in stays, I should blame the first and be inclined to acquit the last, because it is well known that few (especially loaden ships) will *quickly* answer their weather helm; some ships will veer off till they bring the wind abaft the beam, and run with it to a considerable distance; and as by running so far from the wind their velocity will be greatly increased, the greater will be the danger of sinking one or both if they meet. The most prudent method in this

case is, for both ships to put their helms hard down a lee, and then if they should fall along side of each other, they will touch gently, and probably do no damage. There are few mates or masters but know this ought to be done, but they often, and too often fatally, are induced to try the experiment of veering to avoid the trouble of staying their ships. Besides men ought to be deterred from attempting to veer when they suddenly meet with a ship at a small distance from them, from the consideration, that both ships may do the same, and then, if they meet, the crash is dreadful indeed.

5. When ships are working to windward in a narrow channel, with sands on each side, it is more difficult in such a situation to give a right judgment, but the following remarks may serve as rules to judge by. Suppose many ships are turning in the Cockle Gatt, one of them stays as near the Cockle Sand as is prudent to go, a ship following on her weather quarter continues her stretch, intending to tack within her, and runs on board of her and sinks her, or causes her to miss stays and run upon the sand; he is, I think, wholly to blame, as it was in his power to have prevented the damage,

but wholly out of the power of the other to have avoided it. Suppose two of these plying ships meet near mid-channel, as they approach towards each other, that ship which opens the land or any other object to windward, and continues to do so (especially if she have the masts of the other open to windward) has a right to the weather gage; if the other wilfully keep her loof and strike the former, it will be on the lee-side, which is of itself a proof, without other evidence, that he is to blame, and consequently would be liable to pay the greater part of the damage, but not the whole, because a prudent master when he falls in with such a fool-hardy and self-willed man, will throw his ship about, and by that means lessen, if not wholly prevent damage.

6. In turning up rivers much damage is often done, and more through want of care than want of knowledge; the edge of the tide is the rule for putting about, even though the tide does not run half the breadth of the reach. Some imprudently stand out of the tide, and occasion thereby much trouble to themselves and many of the ships in company with them; for when they come out of the eddy, and the edge of the tide

takes their lee bow, it throws them in the wind, and though the helm be hard a-weather, the mizen-sheet flown, or the peak of the main-sail down, she will drive like a log under no command, probably the whole length of the reach: let all others be careful not to stand too near her, for if they do any damage, they must answer the consequences.

These few general rules, carefully observed, would prevent much of the damage that happens at sea; and as every candid person from reading these remarks, must be convinced that none but seamen can be proper judges in case of damage done at sea; is it not in the highest degree absurd, to refer such matters to lawyers, and a jury of merchants and mechanics?

ADDRESS TO SEAMEN, BUT ESPECIALLY TO THE RISING YOUTH.

Those who have used the sea, and have attained the age of forty or fifty years, must have observed a very great declension in all orders of seamen, both with respect to morals and discipline.

Forty-two years ago, when the writer of

this address first went to sea, masters had a great interest in the ships they commanded (being mostly owners, or part owners) and generally had such a high sense of honor, that no hardships or danger appeared to them so formidable, as an imputation on their conduct as seamen. Had they lost a ship, and it was supposed to be owing either to ignorance, or carelessness, it was long before they were intrusted with the charge of another, or could prevail on any to venture friendly parts with them; so that the loss of a ship, in those days, frequently involved the loss of *character* as well as *property*.

Few ship-owners made insurance on policy, and such as did seldom insured half the amount of their interest. Masters at that time observed a respectable and dignified conduct, for though they slept less, and walked the deck more than any of the crew when the ship was at sea, they seldom entered into any unnecessary conversation with the sailors; their mates were their confidents, and to them they committed the entire management of the ship while in port, or in a road-stead at anchor.

As to boys, they were then more obedient to

the men, than they are now to their masters; they never durst go on shore without leave of the mate, and that could seldom be obtained more than once a week, half of them in the forenoon, and the other half in the afternoon; it is needless to say, that they were obliged to be on board at the time appointed.

The oldest apprentice had a sort of delegated authority over his fellow servants, and each one had some part of the ship's stores under his particular care, which he was bound to have in readiness whenever called for; instead of blows and abusive language, mates contrived to substitute shame and degradation, by assigning mean offices to such as were last in turning out, or were otherwise backward or unhandy in doing their duty; such as sweeping the decks, cleaning the boats, &c. to avoid which, the writer has fresh in his recollection the many hard races he has run (upon the mate knocking all hands out) to be among the first at the windlass palls.

To haul out the *weather earing* when the topsails were to reef, to *ship* the first handspike, and to *cat* the anchor, were objects contended for by men and boys, as points of honor.

To such discipline and subordination must be attributed the smallness of the number of ships then lost, compared with what now happens, making every allowance for the increase of shipping.

It is lamentable to think how ships are now thrown away; with sea winds and hazy weather we see them keeping near the land and grappling for harbours, by which many with their crews are lost; when at such times, by keeping the sea a few days longer, they might have prevented such disasters; but what is most astonishing—a master, who looses his ship through ignorance or carelessness, finds little difficulty in obtaining the command of another, without any stigma from the public, or any apparent contrition on his part.

To bring seamen back to that state of vigilance and care, so conspicuous in their forefathers, is the design of this address; and as the future prosperity or calamity of this country will very much depend on the virtues or vices of the rising generation, the writer hopes he need not apologize for earnestly exhorting them to stem the strong current of luxury and dissipation of the present day.

A growing contempt of religion and good morals seem to pervade the far greater part of mankind; and, unless a considerable reformation takes place, inevitable ruin will be the consequence.

Without religion there can be no solid virtue, no good morals, no true honor; all the *apparent* good actions of bad men spring from mean and selfish motives. That ferocity called courage, (too often kept up by artificial means) is, in such men, like that of animals devoid of reason; hence their commands are boisterous, fickle, and confused: in that state of mind there is great danger of their issuing orders, the reverse of what they should do.

Good men encounter difficulties and dangers with rational courage; and such as are commanders, give their orders in a calm, cheerful and dispassionate manner, and their example animates and encourages all that sail with them.

The religion recommended to all (and of which all in every situation are capable) consists in sentiments of piety, and in reflections on the power, providence, and goodness of God, and in actions correspondent therewith.

Such sentiments, and such conduct, would give young men (who have nothing to depend upon but their own merit) the fairest chance of preferment; and if it has been their loss to have had parents who either could not, or would not, give them a suitable education, they will have many opportunities of improvement while at sea and in port.

The famous circumnavigator, Capt. Cook, served his apprenticeship in the coal and coasting trade, and acquired almost all his knowledge of books after he went to sea: he was a striking instance of the power of emulation, united with sobriety and an ardent application; his example is worthy the imitation of every seaman.

Although not in order of time, I hope it will not be deemed improper to mention that having heard from others, and experienced difficulties myself, in disputes relative to insurance cases, and damage done by ships running foul of each other,—in 1793, I called (by an essay in a provincial paper) the attention of the ship-owners, merchants, and underwriters, of the port of Newcastle, to the propriety and necessity of of an association for the purpose of general arbitration.

This was so favourably received, that on the 6th of 6th mo. in said year, a meeting was held and adjourned to the 20th of said month. I was assisted in drawing up the rules and regulations by some friends, and the annexed address was written by that sensible and benevolent man, William Turner, of Newcastle.

" At a general meeting held in the Trinity Hall, Newcastle, on the 20th June, 1793, (being an adjournment of the meeting held the 6th of same month) pursuant to public advertisement.

" Resolved,

" That it is the opinion of this meeting that many great advantages would arise, particularly to the mercantile interests of this country, from the formation and establishment of general associations for promoting the settlement of differences by arbitration.

" That such an association would be particularly useful in this populous trading district, more especially with respect to all disputes relating to shipping and insurance.

" That such an association be now formed under the denomination of the *Newcastle upon Tyne company for general arbitration*.

That this association consist of the following gentlemen, and such others as may afterwards be admitted by ballot.

NEWCASTLE.

T. E. Headlman
George Burdon
R. Lisle
Samuel Lawton
J. Sorsbie
Walter Hall
William Row
William Kent
Malin Sorsbie
Henry Shadforth
George Blaylock
J. J. Davis
L. Atkinson
John Chapman
J. Robinson
Robert Rankin
John Wallis
Robert Yelloley
John Hindmarsh
Thomas Robinson
M. Atkinson
J. Atkinson
Benjamin Brunton
George Shadforth
Radcliffe Manchester
George Tallentire
Thomas Snaith
Thomas Smith
Robert Chapman
George Henderson

NORTH SHIELDS.

John Walker
Q. Blackburn
Thomas Wright
George Brown
Wm. Clark, Sen.
James Smith
Wm. Curry
John Fenwick
John Hearn
John Cunningham

J. Walmsley	George French
Thomas Ware	Wm. Richardson
John Scott	Wm. Clark, Jun.
S. Hurry	Henry Taylor
Mark Willins, Howdon	

SOUTH SHIELDS.

M. Rockwood	Richard Scott
Wm. Masterman	Joseph Bulmer
John Salmon	L. Broderick

" That the company will hold general meetings on the 2d Thursday in June, September, December, and March, to ballot for the admission of members, to receive and examine such questions in dispute as may be referred to them, and to assign the determination of each particular case to such three members as may be deemed best qualified to decide upon it. That the appointment be made by written lists to be given in by each member and scrutinized openly: the three named in most lists to be the arbitrators.

" That in all questions of difference referred to this association the parties deliver their respective cases (if they can agree in one case it will be the most desirable) to the clerk at his office, sealed; and if any are received within the first six weeks from the last general meeting, he is authorized to call a special meeting; but if later they shall lay over to the next general meeting.

" That one guinea be paid by each party to the clerk, on delivering the cases to him; but if one half per cent. on the amount exceed two guineas, one half per cent. shall be paid by the parties on the delivery of the award, in such proportions as the arbitrators shall deem reasonable; in this case the two guineas shall be returned.

" That on the second Thursday in June, in every year, the accounts shall be audited; after paying the clerk's salary, and incidental expenses, the surplus shall be given to charity.

" That the clerk minutely record in a book kept for that purpose, the several cases, with their respective awards, which may have been determined by the arbitrators, together with the reasons on which such awards were grounded.

" That such persons as are desirous of becoming members of this association, are requested to leave their names with the clerk to be reported at the next general or special meeting.

" That notice of this association be published three successive weeks in each of the Newcastle papers; together with the address to the public, which has now been read, and which is fully approved by this meeting,

" That Robert Young, in the High Bridge, Newcastle, is appointed clerk to this association.

" ADDRESS THE PUBLIC.

" The many inconveniences which attend the present mode of obtaining the settlement of disputes, or the redress of grievances in our public courts of law, are matters of universal complaint. This is the case with regard to all law suits; but there are some peculiar grievances which are chiefly felt by the *merchant*, the *insurer*, and the *ship-owner*. The differences which arise among these important classes of the community, are, in our courts of law, almost necessarily referred to incompetent judges. The gentlemen educated for the profession of the law, being usually in no respect qualified to enter into the intricacies of long and complicated accounts; to judge in cases of damage sustained at sea, which, or whether either party has been in fault, and to settle the *quantum* of damages accordingly; or even in many cases to understand so much as the meaning of the terms, in which the matter in dispute must necessarily be related; so that the decisions of the courts, upon cases of this nature, are found to give little satisfaction to the parties concerned, and, not unfrequently excite the ridicule of those whose profession enables them to judge: and, after all, it is often found expedient to refer such matters to the arbitration of persons conversant in the business, when the parties have wearied each other with the expences of repeated suits.

" On these accounts, the method of reference to the arbitration of persons qualified to judge of any particular subject of difference, is, in every respect, preferable to the practice of seeking redress by what is called, " the due course " of law."

" And it will not admit of a dispute, whether it is not better calculated for the preservation of peace and harmony among individuals, that the subjecting of an opponent to the expences of a law suit, and to petulant abuse from the practisers in our courts, which often lay the foundations of animosities that last for life.

" Indeed, experience has so fully shewn the
" great use of these peaceable and domestic
" tribunals, especially in settling matters of
" account, and other mercantile transactions,
" *which are difficult and almost impossible to be*
" *adjusted on a trial at law*, the legislature has
" established the use of them, as well in con-
" troversies where causes are depending, as in
" those where no action is brought; enacting
" by 9 and 10 William the III. c. 15, that all
" merchants and others, who desire to end any
" controversy, suit, or quarrel, for which there
" is no remedy but by personal action, or suit
" in equity, may agree that their submission of
" the suit to arbitration, or umpirage, shall be
" made a rule of in any of the King's courts
" of record, and may insert such agreement in
" their submission, promise, or condition of the
" arbitration bond; which agreement, being
" proved upon oath by one of the witnesses
" thereto, the court shall make a rule that

"such submission and award shall be conclusive."

BLACKSTONE, vol. III. p. 16.

" But although great advantages have arisen from the usual mode of arbitration, yet it is liable to one strong objection, viz. that the arbitrators being chosen by the parties in the dispute, they are too apt to consider themselves rather as the advocates for their respective friends, than as concerned to decide according to truth and justice.

" On these accounts, a number of gentlemen, resident in Newcastle and its neighbourhood, (the nature of whose concerns may be expected to lead them to a particular acquaintance with shipping, insurance, and commerce) have agreed to form themselves into an association for general arbitration, which they hope will be attended with this peculiar advantage, that while it holds out all the other benefits of this method of settling differences, it will provide at the same time, every possible security for impartiality of decision, by the rule which they have adopted for the appointment of arbitrators.

" To the inhabitants of this great commercial district, the association respectfully offer their best services, for the prevention of unnecessary litigation, and the expense and trouble consequent thereupon."

" These decisions were often grievously expensive. They were, besides, frequently different from what seafaring persons conceived to be just. The latter circumstance was attributed to the ignorance of lawyers in maritime affairs. Much money was therefore often expended, and no one satisfied. Some Quakers in the neighbourhood, in conjunction with others, came forward with a view of obviating these evils. They proposed arbitration as a remedy. They met with some opposition at first, but principally from gentlemen of the law. After having, however, shewn the impropriety of many of the legal verdicts that had been given, they had the pleasure of seeing their plan publicly introduced and sanctioned. For in the month of June, 1793, a number of gentlemen, respectable for their knowledge in mercantile and maritime affairs, met at the Trinity-hall in Newcastle, and associated themselves for these and other purposes, calling themselves

The Newcastle-upon Tyne association for general arbitration."

" This association was to have four general meetings in the year, one in each quarter, at which they were to receive cases. For any urgent matter, however, which might occur, the clerk was to have the power of calling a special meeting.

" Each person, on delivering a case, was to pay a small fee. Out of these fees the clerk's salary and incidental expences were to be paid. But the surplus was to be given to the poor.

" The parties were to enter into arbitration bonds, as is usual upon such occasions.

" Each party was to choose out of this association, or standing committee, one arbitrator for himself, and the association were to choose or to ballot for a third. And here it will be proper to observe, that this standing association appeared to be capable of affording arbitrators equal to the determination of every case. For, if the matter in dispute between the two parties were to happen to be a mercantile question, there were merchants in the association. If a question relative to shipping, there were ship-owners in it. If a question of insurance, there were insurance-brokers also. A man could hardly fail of having his case determined by persons who were competent to the task.

" Though this beautiful institution was thus publicly introduced, and introduced with considerable expectations and applause, cases came in but slowly. Custom and prejudice are not to be rooted out in a moment. In process of time, however, several were offered, considered, and decided, and the presumption was, that the institution would have grown with time. Of those cases, which were determined, some relating to ships, were found to be particularly intricate, and cost the arbitrators considerable time and trouble. The verdicts, however, which were given, were in all of them satisfactory. The institution at length became so popular, that, incredible to relate, its own popularity destroyed it! So many persons were ambitious of the honour of becoming members of the committee, that some of inferior knowledge and judgment, and character, were too hastily admitted into it. The consequence was, that people dared not trust their affairs to the abilities of every member, and the institution expired, after having rendered important services to numerous individuals, who had tried it.

"When we consider that this institution has been tried, and that the scheme of it has been found practicable, it is a pity that its benefits should have been confined, and this for so short a period, to a single town. Would it not be desirable, if, in every district, a number of farmers were to give in their names to form a standing committee, for the settlement of disputes between farmer and farmer? or that there should be a similar institution among manufacturers, who should decide between one manufacturer and another? Would it not also be desirable, if, in every parish, a number of gentlemen, or other respectable persons, were to associate for the purpose of accommodating the differences of each other? For this beautiful system is capable of being carried to any extent, and of being adapted to all stations and conditions of life. By these means numerous little funds might be established in numerous districts, from the surplus of which an opportunity would be afforded of adding to the comforts of such of the poor as were to distinguish themselves by their good behaviour, whether as labourers for farmers, manufacturers, or others. By these means, also, many of the quarrels in parishes might be settled to the mutual satisfaction of the parties concerned, and in so short a space of time as to prevent them from contracting a rancorous and a wounding edge. Those, on the other hand, who were to assist in these arbitrations, would be amply repaid; for they would be thus giving an opportunity of growth to the benevolent feelings, and they would have the pleasing reflection, that the tendency of their labours would be to promote peace and good-will amongst men."

I am now entered into the seventy-fourth year of my age, and can with some degree of satisfaction take a retrospective view of my past life. I attribute all the good I may be supposed to have done to the superintendance and guidance of Divine Providence.

I console myself with the pleasing thought, that long after I have gone to "*where the wicked cease from troubling, and the weary are at rest;*" the generous sailor running through Hasboro' Gatt, in a dark night and northerly wind, will feel thankful to Almighty goodness for making Henry Taylor the instrument of giving him such consoling lights.

An abstract of the Royal Charter, and acts of parliament granted to the master, wardens, and elder brethren of the Trinity House, Deptford Strond, relating to ballastage, beaconage, buoyage, and pilotage.

6th of Henry the VIII. 1515, the charter of incorporation was granted, with power and authority to hold lands and tenements of the value of 20 marks a year.

1556, the 8th of Elizabeth, entitled an act to enable the Trinity House to erect sea-marks.

After that various ancient sea-marks on land had been cut or fallen down, it empowers the Trinity House to set up marks for the governance of ships at sea, and that all such beacons, marks, and signs, set up *at the cost and charges of the said master, wardens, elder brethren, or assistants*, shall and may be continued and renewed *at the cost and charge of the said master, &c.*

36th of Elizabeth, 1594, a royal grant of the ballastage, beaconage, and buoyage, was granted to the Trinity House.

The preamble that C. Lord Howard, was by virtue of letters patent as Admiral of England, entitled to the exclusive right of ballasting all ships or vessels sailing into or out of the River Thames, and also, of erecting, setting up, placing, and laying out of all, or any beacons, marks, buoys, or signs of the sea, &c. yet it did notwithstanding appear to him, that it is in, and by, one act of parliament made in the 8th year of her said Majesty's reign, specified, and expressed, ordained and enacted, that the said master wardens, and assistants, should from time to time, at their will and pleasures, and at *their costs and charges*, make and set up beacons marks, and signs, &c. in consideration thereof and divers other causes, him therein moving the said great Admiral of England, did beseech her said Majesty, to permit him to resign the right, that he possesed by the said letters patent, so far as related to the ballasting, beaconage, and buoyage, and that the said right might be assigned to the master wardens and assistants.

In compliance with this request, her said Majesty, did give, grant, confirm, and ratify to the said master and assistants, the above rights.

17th of Charles the II. 1665, a royal grant of ballastage, to the Trinity House.

By this act they were bound to provide a sufficient number of lighters for ballasting ships, at the price then accustomed.

1st of James the II. 1685, the royal charters including regulations respecting pilots, and they are authorized to make sundry bye-laws, " provided always *that the said laws, ordinances,* " *and statutes be not repugnant to the laws,* " *statues, rights, or customs of this our realm of* " *England,*" derogatory to the jurisdiction or pre-eminence of the Lord High Admiral of England for the time being, or the court of Admiralty.

5th of George II. 1732, an act of parliament, entitled, an act for the better regulation and government of pilots, in the River Thames, Medway, &c. It concludes, " And further " that this act shall not extend to the taking " away, or any wise abridging any grants or " other privileges, heretofore possessed by " the Trinity House of Kingston upon Hull, " the Trinity House of Newcastle upon Tyne,

" or the Trinity Houses of Dover, Deal, or the " Isle of Thanet."

By an act of parliament, made in the 3d of George the II. which act, under various renewals, continues in force until the 25th June, 1806, " and from thence to the end of " the next sessions of parliament."

6th of George II. fixes the price of ballast: it had been nine-pence per ton for colliers, twelve-pence all other British ships, and sixteen-pence per ton for foreign ships. By this act the price was raised to twelve-pence colliers, fifteen-pence other British ships, and nineteen-pence foreigners, *and no more*, which said act, under various renewals, shall continue in force until the 25th June, 1806.

N. B. the above act expressly says, the said rates cannot be increased without *authority of parliament*.

The foregoing abstracts contain the material parts of the Royal Charters and acts of parliament, whereby the master, wardens, and assistants of the Trinity House Deptford Strond are incorporated.

Taking a review of the same, so far as relates to the establishing of beacons, marks, and signs, of the sea, neither the act of parliament, which was made in the 8th year of Queen Elizabeth, nor the grant made in the 26th year of that reign, nor any other grant yet published, established any legal right in the Trinity House to impose a toll or duty on any ship, or other vessel, for the purpose of defraying the expence of placing beacons, buoys, &c. but merely directs that the said master, wardens, and assistants, shall place the same at *their* own *costs* and *charges*, this service can be considered in no other point of view, than that of enabling the corporation to perform the duty they had solicited (by loads, manage, pilotage, and primage,) with due safety, and for which the exclusive privilege enjoyed was to be considered the recompence.

As the Term *light houses*, does not present itself, it is reasonable to presume that no such establishment was then in the contemplation of the Trinity House, much less *floating lights*, which were not placed in any situation until a late period. The words beacons and buoys, it is admitted, have furnished the Trinity House with a colourable pretext for placing light houses and floating lights, but in all cases where the establishment of such lights requires the imposition of a toll or duty upon the public for their support, it as much exceeds the legal powers of the corporation to force such an establishment, as to construct a canal, excavate a dock, or any other work whatever which may require the levying a duty for its maintenance.

The first floating light on the East Coast, was that placed near the Dodgeon Shoal in the Deeps.

Ship-owners from various losses had seen the necessity of such a light; the Trinity House would not comply with their wishes, but agreed that such ship-owners might place one there at their *own cost* and *charges*, and receive one penny per chaldron on colliers, and the same per ton on merchant ships. Accordingly about one hundred years ago (as I am informed) a few gentlemen of Whitby, of the names of Walker, Chapman, Stockton, and Kitchingman, did place and maintain the said light. At first it did not produce much profit, but as the trade increased, it became more productive; when the Trinity House took it from the original owners, and have continued ever since to charge one penny per chaldron, and one penny per ton; although, from the vast increase of shipping, one farthing would be more than sufficient for its maintenance.

The usual mode formerly has been to grant acts of parliament to individuals who had projected sea lights, but of *late* years the corporation of the Trinity House have assumed an exclusive right, and, unauthorized by parliament, have placed such lights, and have imposed on the public, through the medium of the shipping interest, exorbitant tolls and duties for their maintenance.

To persons unacquainted with the manner of forming those establishments, it may be proper to observe, that as soon as a project of a new light is perfected, the Trinity House transmit to the different sea-ports of the kingdom, a requisition, stating therewith, that the light will be placed when the signatures of the ship-owners and merchants are procured, and the requisition paper returned to them.

At a convenient time, after this preliminary process, the light is placed in the situation proposed, and is immediately followed by an *impost* upon those ship-owners, who have signed, and upon *all others* using those seas; but it is contended, that the consent of a part cannot bind the aggregate body at all times present and *forever*. And, further, that such a proceeding is repugnant to the laws of the realm, which allows of no impost, without the sanction of the legislature; and for this, is adduced, the practice of the Trinity House itself, in the instances of ballastage and pilotage, for both of which acts of parliament have been procured, to enable the corporation to provide for the expences which eventually attend the same, notwithstanding the original grants to the Trinity House, authorised the receipt of the then usual dues in both these cases.

The placing the light houses near Hasboro' Church, and the floating light near the Newarp Sand, on the coast of Norfolk, in the year 1789, the floating light at the north-end of the Goodwin Sand, on the coast of Kent, and the floating light at the east-end of the Sunk Sand, on the coast of Essex, in the year 1795, are offered in evidence of the above statement.

P. S. The above lights which have contributed in an eminent degree to the safety of shipping and commerce, and have also preserved to their country the valuable lives of great numbers of seamen, are very amply supported; but the individual who, with incessant labour for several years, and at an heavy expense, planned and matured these important projects, remains without a remuneration, in any degree commensurate to the services he has rendered his country.

Extract of a letter from the person who procured from the Patent Office, the account of the foregoing charters, &c. of the corporation of the Trinity House.

" I have made inquiry at the Patent Office
" and there am acquainted, that the King
" posseses the right of granting licenses, im-
" posing tolls upon the subjects of Great-
" Britain; but this part of the prerogative is
" rarely made use of, there having been but
" two instances (and those merely renewals of
" grants) since the year 1739, except to the
" Trinity House, who have procured various

" such grants; those can only be procured by
" high interest at court; and this accounts for
" the policy of the Trinity House electing into
" their honourable situations men great in
" power.

" The proposed inquiry will, no doubt, lead
" to an envelopement of some mysterious con-
" duct.

" I have generally understood, that at the
" Revolution the King accepted the crown
" under an assurance, that such parts of the
" prerogatives as his successors had enjoyed,
" and which were inimical to the profits of the
" people, should be forever revoked. There
" must have been some declaration to establish
" the term."

FINIS.

www.ingramcontent.com/pod-product-compliance
Lightning Source LLC
LaVergne TN
LVHW061310060426
835507LV00019B/2084